Contents

REAL BOOKS *for* READING

Learning to Read *with* Children's Literature

LINDA HART-HEWINS and JAN WELLS

Pembroke Publishers Limited

For William – the reader who helped us learn together.

Pembroke Publishers Limited
528 Hood Road
Markham Ontario L3R 3K9

Canadian Cataloguing in Publication Data
Hart-Hewins, Linda
    Real books for reading : learning to read with children's literature

Includes bibliographical references.
ISBN 0-921217-55-2

1. Reading (Primary) - Language experience approach.
2. Children - Books and reading. I. Wells, Jan.
1948-   . II. Title.

LB1525.34H37 1990   372.4'044   C90-0905063-3

Published in U.S.A. by
Heinemann Educational Books Inc.
361 Hanover Street
Portsmouth, NH 03801-3959

Library of Congress Cataloguing-in-Publication Data
Hart-Hewins, Linda
    Real books for reading: learning to read with children's
    literature / Linda Hart Hewins and Jan Wells.
        p.   cm.
    Includes bibliographical references.
    ISBN 0-435-08547-6
        1. Reading (Primary) 2. Children–Books and reading.
3. Classroom environment. 4. Language arts (Primary) I. Wells,
Jan. II. Title.
LB1525.H27 1990
372.6'4--dc20
                                                            90-43145
                                                            CIP

Editor: Quantum Leap Communications
Design: Falcom Design and Communications Inc.
Cover photography by David Street

Printed and bound in Canada by Webcom Limited
0 9 8 7 6 5 4 3 2

Acknowledgments

We owe a great deal to other writers and teachers who have helped shape our practice. We are particularly grateful to Donald Graves and Nancie Atwell for showing us how to listen to children and respond to their ideas. Bob Barton and David Booth have given us ways to see inside the stories and explore them. Judy Sarick and her staff at The Children's Bookstore in Toronto offered us both time and assistance in selecting books from their carefully chosen collection. Teacher-librarians, especially Marge Kelly, Gloria Lasciewicz, and Ann Diakiw have shared their knowledge of children's literature with us. We are grateful to many colleagues who have shared ideas and listened to us with patience. In particular we thank Maxine Bone, Anna Greig, Jane Milliken, Anne Smythe, Val Taylor and Una Villiers whose commitment to children and learning has been an inspiration. Writers too numerous to mention have given us stories to share with our children. But most important of all are the children it has been our privilege to teach and from whom we have learned so much.

Introduction

"Reading like learning to swim takes hours of practice, but the practice must be in a real book that gives as much personal satisfaction as plunging in the cold water of a lake gives to the swimmer."

Charlotte Huck[1]

Using Real Books in the Classroom. What Are the Components of the Program?

This book is the result of a collaboration over a number of years in which we have put into practice our growing conviction that children need real books and real writing experiences to become fluent and enthusiastic readers. We have tried to create a language program that focuses not on the print but on stories – a program in which it is what you can *do* with language that matters. By discovering stories and writers, we have learned something of the power of the written word and its potential for enhancing learning; through the use of real books in our classrooms, we have helped children to become not only literate but also lovers of reading. In Grade 2 David wrote in his reading journal, "*Miss Rumphius* is my favorite book of all the books in our collection because she wants to make the world a more beautiful place." He understands not only *how* to read but also *why* we read, and that is the goal of our language program.

We have written this book for teachers of young children who wish to implement a literature-based reading and writing program in their classrooms. It may be of help to administrators and parents who want to understand more about the way that young children are being taught to read in kindergarten and the first three grades. It offers practical guidelines for organizing a classroom that fosters the growth of reading and writing in an atmosphere that values play, hands-on activities, and the arts. It respects the child's need for ownership and for time to complete self-chosen tasks.

NOTE

We refer to our own classrooms throughout the book. Linda's class is a family group of kindergarten and Grade 1 students; Jan's is a family group of Grade 1 and 2 students.

---

[1]Charlotte Huck, "Literature as the Content of Reading," *Theory Into Practice*, vol. 26 (The Ohio State University, 1987), p. 375.

Using real books in the language program classroom involves children working individually, with partners, in small groups, and in the whole-class setting. We focus on activities from which we expect specific learning about reading and writing to emerge. All of these activities involve teaching and learning about stories and writers. Very few of them involve teaching about parts of words or components of sentences. None of them involve teaching about language, letters, and words outside the meaningful context of some other activity.

In the chapters that follow we will describe ten essential ingredients for a successful language program. Briefly summarized, these are:

1. There Are Real Books in the Classroom

The classroom contains a wide variety of reading materials, at the heart of which is a collection of stories from which the children choose. This collection is kept fresh by borrowing from the school library and by the replacement of worn-out books. Children also have daily access to the larger collection in the school's library resource centre. The bibliography in this book offers teachers a starting point for selecting books for primary classrooms.

2. The Teacher Shares Books With Individuals

The teacher shares books with individual children on a regular basis, encouraging them in their efforts and helping them to develop strategies to unlock the author's meaning; helping them in their choices of books; and discussing their responses and ideas. The teacher keeps anecdotal records in the child's reading log as a routine part of these reading times.

3. The Teacher Reads Aloud Every Day

Stories are read aloud by the teacher to the class. Sometimes, but not every time, discussion follows and suggestions for possible projects related to that story are exchanged. Sometimes a story reading becomes a joint activity, especially if a big book or poetry on a chart is used.

4. Children Have Time to Read Alone or With a Friend

The children read by themselves and to other children from self-selected books made freely available in a comfortable setting. They record their reading in their reading log. Very young children can draw a picture or an adult can maintain their record for them. This log becomes a cumulative record of books enjoyed at school.

5. Borrow a Book

The children borrow books from the school library and from the classroom to take home. Parents are encouraged to share home reading experiences with their children and are invited to make a comment about the book on a special card or in a record book.

6. Buddy Reading

The children hear stories read aloud to them by other students and adults within the school. They engage in discussion about those reading experiences and note their responses in a record book or on a comment card.

7. Children Have Time to Write

The children write daily about topics of their own choosing. Story making may be inspired by and modelled on the texts shared in the reading program. Writing also takes place in play situations in the classroom.

8. Response to Stories Takes Many Forms

Children engage in activities that expand the meaning of the stories they have shared. They may retell them, tape-record their own versions, sing, dance, or act them out, or represent them by making puppets, constructions of various types, paintings, or drawings.

9. Reading and Writing Are Part of Play

The children read and write as part of every activity in which they are engaged–reading signs and instructions, writing labels and notices. They are encouraged to notice ways in which reading and writing are used in the real world and to include them in their play whenever possible.

10. Reading and Writing Are Part of All Learning

Whenever topics or themes of interest are pursued in the classroom, stories and poems that relate to the theme are shared. Collections of thematically linked books are placed in a theme centre. Ideas for special activities suggested by these books are discussed. Themes often start with the reading of a book and activities are brainstormed and developed by the children. Whenever children have interests or ideas that they wish to pursue, there is a book or a story to be found that relates to the situation.

These then are the ten components of the program. Before we begin our exploration of these in depth, we will first review the reasons *why* we teach this way, and relate our practice to theory and experience.

Chapter 1

"Reading Takes You to Other Worlds"

Why Do We Use Real Books?

My Grade 2 students had been with me for two years. For two years we had shared stories together. At the end of the summer term I asked them to write an answer to the following question: "What do you think reading is?" Here are some of their responses.

> "Reading is fun," wrote Kimmy. "You get to read good stories."
> "Reading helps you learn," wrote Jeff.
> "Reading makes you use your imagination," said Rajesh.
> "Reading a book is a good way to pass the time," wrote Alison.
> "Reading helps you spell better," was Ricky's comment.

Perhaps the most perceptive remark of all came from Jason, who captured the essence and power of the reading experience when he wrote, "Reading takes you to other worlds."

While we believe in using literature-based reading programs throughout the school, our suggestions are specifically aimed at those teachers who have the job of teaching reading to the youngest children. These teachers have a tremendous responsibility. During these early years the children are expected to learn *how* to read, to crack the written code. We know that we don't actually teach children to read. We only facilitate their learning, and children know this, too. One little girl very indignantly told her father, "Mrs. Wells didn't teach me to read, I taught myself!"

The suggestions we offer are deeply rooted in some fundamental beliefs about how children learn and how they learn language in particular. In this chapter we present the arguments that have led us to adopt our current practices.

What Do We Know About Language Learning?

The first thing we have discovered about language learning is that it takes place because the learner is seeking to achieve other goals. We don't deliberately set out to learn language, either spoken or written; we acquire language in the pursuit of other activities, as a means of realizing other purposes. It is a tool for learning, but of course the more we use it to seek other knowledge or achieve other goals, the more competent we become as language users. Reading is one of the ways in which we learn about experience – our own and others'. Through reading we see how writers have represented experience. We also gain access to knowledge outside or beyond our direct experience. Remember, reading takes you to other worlds! And in the process of reading to learn, we learn how to read.

We want children to learn to love reading and to become lifelong readers, to have access to the world through books. To want to read, they must see the point of it. Motivation to learn is a key factor in their language acquisition. In language learning the function of the language is always mastered before the form. We discover what language can do and then we determine that we will master it. Children must first discover the power of writing so that they will want to read and write for themselves.

Teachers have to communicate a love of reading to their students so that they will want to crack the code. The most important role of teachers in the language program is to demonstrate through their own reading and writing that they value literacy and literature. We do not teach children to read, they teach themselves; we can only motivate, encourage, and guide the learning. Margaret Meek says:

"To learn to read, children need the attention of one patient adult, or an older child, for long enough to read something that pleases them both. A book, a person, and shared enjoyment: these are the conditions of success."[2]

We have also learned that language learning is a meaning-making process that begins at birth and continues in the world outside the school regardless of the practices of the school. Children become competent users of their first language without any formal teaching. Speaking, listening, reading, and writing are social as well as cognitive events, and they are driven by the child's inherent curiosity and urge to make sense of things. Children seek explanations and connections. They want to do what others around them do, to have the competencies of their older brothers and sisters, of parents and friends. Frank Smith has called the community of users of written language a "literacy club"[3] and it is this club that young children want to join.

In the world outside the school, people use language to get things done. They write notes to each other, exchange letters, compile lists, and read recipes, instructions, and manuals. They read for pleasure: magazines, newspapers, and books. They read signs and advertisements for information. Children are great imitators; they copy the behavior of the adults around them. William at three wrote scribbles on tiny pieces of paper which he gave to his toys as tickets for the bus. Tara watched her father write out cheques at the supermarket; later he found her with the chequebook writing out her own! Even very young children notice signs in the environment. When her family was passing a Mac's Milk store Megan, age two and a half, said, "Look, Mummy, there's my M!"

Language users begin with intentions and purposes and use language to realize those intentions. This is the environment in which children learn to be competent users of their first spoken language before they begin school. It is this environment that enables children to learn a great deal about the written code before they ever have a lesson on the subject and to become efficient readers before they ever meet a reading book. Young children learn that print carries meaning, that it makes sense, and that it does something useful. They *expect* language to be meaningful.

---

[2] Margaret Meek, *Learning to Read* (London: The Bodley Head, 1982), p.9.
[3] Frank Smith, *Reading Without Nonsense* (New York: Teachers College Press, 1985), p. 123.

Traditionally, this background knowledge about language which all children possess has been ignored by our schools. A new subject is presented to them: reading and writing, sometimes called language arts. This has little to do with the real uses of language with which the children are familiar. It has little to do with what we know about the way that language is learned, in collaboration with others and in interactive situations. It has little to do with what we know about the reading process, which is an active meaning-making process. Instead, reading and writing become concerned with the mastery of small items of linguistic information: letters, sounds, blends, words. The act of reading a real book becomes the goal that can be achieved only when a number of subskills are in place. Like a carrot before a donkey, good books and exciting stories are held out to the children as something to be striven for, something that must be won by hard work. This can be a disconcerting experience for the child from a literate home who is accustomed to the joy of reading. For the child who has not yet experienced very much of the pleasure of stories and books, it is unlikely to convince them that reading is anything they want to be involved with.

Our classroom program has developed in the belief that we can and must recreate in the school environment the conditions of learning that are encountered in the real world. **Reading and writing must be authentic acts for genuine purposes.**

For example, Liam wanted to leave a structure in the block corner so that he could return to it next day. He left the following messages.

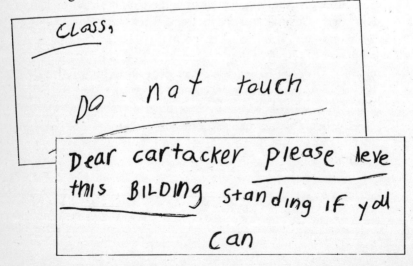

The writing shows us that Liam knows that notices can both request compliance and give orders. Interestingly, he orders his classmates not to touch but politely requests the caretaker to leave the building standing. He already has a sense of audience and register.

William offered this letter to the tooth fairy in lieu of an actual tooth, to ensure that he still received his due reward– a very real concern for William.

> Dear tooth fairy
> two nights ago I lost my tooth and now I
> canot find it. Please accept this note as a
> substitute. From William,
> the owner of the tooth.

Amy and her friends were working to make a restaurant at the dramatic play centre. This is the menu they came up with.

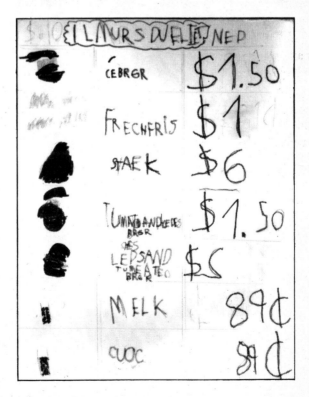

When Gus, a kindergarten boy, was the waiter, he wrote down an order like this:

A pizza
with
tomato
and cheese

The menu designed by the Grade 2 girls on another occasion is somewhat more sophisticated. We can get a really good deal on lobster dinners at their restaurant!

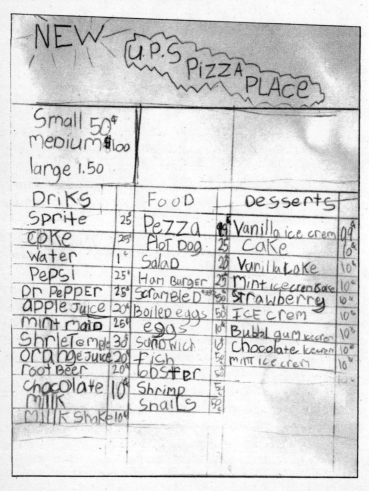

The classroom contexts in which these pieces of writing were generated allowed the children to use written language for their own authentic purposes. For children to see reading as purposeful, it too must arise from a genuinely felt desire.

As teachers we therefore begin with the premise that *choice* of reading material is essential for young readers. We believe that the children themselves are the best judges of which book is the right book for them at any particular time. We think that they know what it is they want to learn. Children learning to read need to be able to choose from a wide range of material. They must be offered the opportunity to find the books that suit their needs, their personality, their interests, and their learning style. The teacher is a facilitator, someone who can make reading suggestions, give encouragement, and make connections for the learner. Teachers and teacher-librarians have a critical role to play in helping create resources from which the children will select their reading material.

What Do We Know About the Reading Process?

Our conviction that the most successful way to learn to read is by reading language that is naturally composed is supported by socio-psycholinguistic theories of reading development. The work of Kenneth and Yetta Goodman, Frank Smith, Don Holdaway, and Constance Weaver, among many others, has illuminated our understanding of reading.

The act of reading is an interaction between three cuing systems, operating simultaneously in a social or situational context.

The *semantic* cuing system involves the reader's common-sense knowledge of what words mean. What do they refer to in the real world? The use of this information depends upon the reader's schema, that is, his or her previous experience of the concepts involved. The context in which the words occur is crucial to this understanding. Kenneth Goodman calls the act of reading "a psycholinguistic guessing game"[4] in which the reader makes predictions and confirms these by reference to the text. Thus, when we see a sign on the door of a store we may predict that it will say Entrance or Exit, Open or Closed. If it is only

[4]Kenneth Goodman, "Reading: A Psycholinguistic Guessing Game," *Journal of the Reading Specialist*, vol. 6, 1967, pp. 26-35.

eight o'clock in the morning we probably guess that it says Closed. We apply our common-sense knowledge of stores and the way they operate, or our schema for stores. Obviously this has implications for the reading that young children can accomplish independently. If they have no experience of a word and the concept to which it refers, they will find it harder to read that word.

We noticed repeatedly that beginning readers tackling John Stadler's book ***Hooray for Snail!*** would invariably make the same miscue. Where the text says, "Snail slams the ball," they read, "Snail hits the ball," despite the visual information to the contrary. We wondered why this should be and then realized that the semantic cuing system was taking precedence over the grapho-phonic. This is because the story has reached the point where the snail is up to bat. The picture shows him hitting the ball. The word "slams" is not the obvious one for this concept. The semantic cues from the story and the picture, together with the child's schema for bats and balls, leads to the miscue nine times out of ten. Children paying close attention to phonics will stall at the word "slams" and be unable to continue.

The second of the cuing systems is the syntactic, which depends upon the reader's knowledge of the spoken language. Syntax is the way in which words are combined in a language to make sense. Subconsciously, all speakers of a language have mastery of the syntax of that language. They know without needing to articulate the knowledge that nouns, verbs, adjectives and adverbs, prepositions, and conjunctions have to be combined in a certain order in a sentence. English speakers do not have to be taught that word order is fundamental to meaning in English. "The boy ate the big peach" makes sense syntactically, but "Boy the ate peach big" does not. As we read, our uncertainty about the text is constantly reduced as the range of syntactic possibilities in any particular position in a sentence is limited. This has implications for second-language learners, as their control of this cuing system is less automatic than that of a native speaker.

It has been our experience that the small function words in a sentence, words such as *and, the, a, at, but,* and *so,* prove to be the hardest for young children to learn by sight, because there are no concepts on which to hook the words. It is also the case that function words, while they are short and appear frequently in all text, are almost redundant in the reading process. A sentence with function words removed is still readable; the eye hardly needs to see these words. Our knowledge of syntax allows us to fill in the conjunctions and prepositions, the definite and indefinite articles. When young children are reading to us and hesitate on these little words, we always fill them in quickly, because we don't want the reader to lose the flow of the language by struggling to sound out these words at the expense of meaning. Function words soon become automatic for the children through constant practise in their daily writing. Because they are high-frequency words, they will be spelled over and over again and eventually recognized when encountered in reading. The syntactic cuing system becomes noticeable when it is *not* used – when a child guesses that a word does not make sense grammatically. As a means of getting meaning from print, it never operates in isolation from the other two cuing systems, the semantic and the grapho-phonic. There is a constant interaction among all three.

The third cuing system is the grapho-phonic. Traditionally it has been assumed that children need mastery of phonics to learn how to read. A large amount of time is still spent in many classrooms teaching phonic rules. There are so many of these that no one, not even the most successful and fluent readers, can articulate them all. In English there are more exceptions to the rules of sound-symbol correspondence than there are regularities. The evidence of young fluent readers who have never had a phonics lesson in their lives disproves the assumption that we need phonics as the basis for learning to read. However, the letters occurring in the first part of a word are important. The first letter of a word, usually a consonant, triggers the reader to bring together the other cuing systems and to make meaning. In other words, children need to know the alphabet. When they encounter an unknown word they need to look at the pictures, think about the story, ask themselves what would make sense, and use the first letters of the word as a springboard to the meaning. When reading the opening lines of Eric Carle's **The Very Hungry Caterpillar,** "In the light of the moon a little egg lay on a leaf," there are very few children who read "In the light of the sun" even though it makes perfect sense. The letter M precludes the word, and as the picture has a face it must be the moon. The semantic and syntactic information is confirmed by the letter cue.

The twenty-six letters of the alphabet are learned in a variety of ways. For many children this learning takes place in the home and the preschool through games such as I Spy, through the writing of family names, and through recognition of letters in the environment. In the classroom the alphabet is quickly mastered through daily reading and writing. During the process of inventing their own spellings, children are forced to draw upon their alphabetic knowledge. Daily writing is therefore a key component of our reading program. Through writing, the children come to know as much about phonics as they need for reading. We discuss the writing program further in chapter six.

The act of reading is far more complex than a simple sounding out of letters. It is an act of construction, of building meanings. To call it decoding is to describe it inaccurately, for it is more constructive than the word implies. Constance Weaver has described the interaction between reader and text as "an ever fluctuating dance that occurs more or less simultaneously on and across various levels: letters, words, sentences, schemata; writer, text and reader; text/reader and context; the present reader with other readers, past and present; and so forth; all connected in a multi-dimensional holarchy, an interlocking network or web of meaning, a synchronous dance..."[5]

This brings us inevitably to the rejection of methods that attempt to teach parts of words and words out of context. It leads us to a belief in children as the best judges of what makes a good book for them. It means that we must have a wide range of reading material, fiction and nonfiction, in our classrooms. For if fluent readers use the three cuing systems together in interaction, then it is clearly nonsense to provide text for beginning readers that bars their access to two-thirds of the available information. **A child's first reading book must make sense and offer as much contextual and syntactic support as possible.** Even fluent readers stumble and miscue their way through print that has no virtue beyond its phonic regularity. Try reading this

---

[5] Constance Weaver, *Reading Process and Practice: From Socio-Psycholinguistics to Whole Language* (Portsmouth, N.H.: Heinemann, 1988).

example from Lippincott's Basic Reading (Book A, 1975).

> Pam ran up the ramp.
> Up the ramp ran the pup.
> The pup and Pam nap.

The model of language acquisition upon which this is based supposes that language can be learned from its component parts to its meaningful whole, rather like adding more and more bricks to a wall until the building is finished. It supposes that children need to master by memory and practise many small items of linguistic information. The children are presented with the sounds of the letters, out of context and for no purpose outside the exercise. These must be memorized. The letters build into words. In order to do this the act of blending the sounds must be mastered. These words can now build into sentences. Naturally such activities are made easier for the learner if they start with simple sounds and easy words. Hence the creation of the preprimer with its litany of short vowel sounds and the ludicrous antics of rats, cats, mats, and hats. Such text not only lacks interest, it is devoid of intelligence. It also prevents the child from using two-thirds of the information that is usually available to readers when they process print. Confronted with this type of writing, young children will try to tell a story about the characters and scenes in the pictures. They cannot predict what the words actually say from these clues.

Books in which the language is predictable both semantically and syntactically offer the maximum support to the early reader. Look again at the opening lines of Eric Carle's **The Very Hungry Caterpillar** :

> In the light of the moon a little egg lay on a leaf. One
> Sunday morning the warm sun came up and — pop!
> — out of the egg came a very small and very hungry
> caterpillar. He started to look for some food.

The picture of the moon, the egg, and the leaf provides a context in which to set the story and so assist the child's attempt to read the words. The logic of the story also provides an internal context. What comes out of eggs on leaves? And what else would a hungry caterpillar do except start to look for food? We find that most children can read the story of *The Very Hungry Caterpillar* with very little practice. The text itself teaches them and the story as it unfolds provides the motivation to read. The rhythm of the language supports the reader and offers confirmation of expectations. The days of the week follow one after the other; numbers increase in order from one to five as the pages turn; and after each feed, the caterpillar "...was still hungry!" The pictures fill the pages with light and color. Real holes are made as the caterpillar "chews" his way through the book, which appeals to the curiosity and sense of discovery of the childen who turn the pages eagerly to find him emerging from the fruits. There is no need to teach them to turn the pages in order. Finally, children can identify with the caterpillar's encounter with too many rich foods, leading to: "That night he had a stomach ache."

The experience of reading this book does not compare with Pam and her pup. It is a *literary* experience as well as an act of reading. It is worth doing for its own sake and there is an ultimate satisfaction in it. The books we use in school should be similar to the books that children read at home, and the interactions that they have with books in school should mirror the genuine acts of reading that take place outside the school. If children learn about language in the home through interaction with adults who do real things with language in everyday contexts, then it is clearly nonsense for schools to try to teach about language in contexts which lack purpose and with texts that are unnaturally constructed. The language activities that go on in classrooms should involve finding information, using instructions, writing messages, keeping records and recording observations, making lists and reading them, sharing reactions to stories, and creating our own stories to share with others.

The sort of storybooks that are shared at home and loved by children and parents alike are the sort of books that should be available in classrooms. The sort of stories that are to be found at the public library are the sort of stories that should be found in school. The things that are done with those books should closely mirror the genuine purposes for which books are intended. Books give pleasure and knowledge. The communal reading of them brings members of families into contact and builds a store of shared experience. Some of the patterns and memories of family life revolve around the times when adults read to children.

Not all children have parents who read to them from children's books. These parents are not worse parents than those who do read, but they are missing a great opportunity to get to know their child and to share enjoyable times together. The children who come to school without previous experience of books and stories need to be introduced to the experience of hearing stories read aloud. They need to see that there are advantages to being members of the literacy club. They will not see that need if the texts they meet are boring and meaningless.

There is another argument, perhaps the most important, for using real books in the early-reading program. We use real books because we want to foster a love of reading. Unless they want to read, children won't read. Unless they gain satisfaction and joy from the act of reading, they will see it as a chore. If it is a chore they will not become lifelong readers.

Literature is not simply a means of entertaining and amusing children. It is essential nourishment for their imaginations, their hearts, and their minds. It contributes to their personal growth by widening their horizons, giving them experiences of people and places out of time and out of space, long ago and far away, here and now but different from themselves. It gives them experiences of personal confirmation when the child in the book is a child with thoughts and fears, adventures and misadventures like their own. It gives them experiences of profound emotional and psychological power. It helps them make sense of their own experience and the experiences of others. People who enjoy reading may not be better human beings, but they are aware that they have access to a range of feelings and experiences that would not otherwise be available to them. When questioned, most adult readers acknowledge that they came to the love of reading during childhood.

Literature which has integrity explores the human experience. It orders and evaluates it, illuminates its heights and depths, gives us images to think with and metaphors for living. Children who do not come to a love of reading miss this essentially humanizing experience. Michele Landsberg writes that: "The adult who takes the time to learn something of children's books and to pass them on with enthusiasm and care gives something precious to the child – and gives something priceless to the world: a child deep rooted in language and story, a child with an educated heart." [6]

Paul Hazard puts it metaphorically: "Give us books, say the children, give us wings." [7]

Finally, we use literature in the reading program because it works. We see children becoming successful readers and learning much more than a system for decoding the basal reader for that grade. We hear children talking about their favorite authors or the way that a story can make you feel creepy or sad. They talk about the way that it's not fair that E.B. White never tells you what happened to Margoles in the story of **Stuart Little,** and that **John Brown, Rose and the Midnight Cat** is about being jealous, "like when you have a new baby." We hear them recommend books to each other. We see them learn to discriminate between books that leave you wondering, like those of Chris Van Allsburg and Maurice Sendak, and those that leave nothing to the imagination. They develop favorites and return to the same book again and again.

Children who learn to read with real books begin to think like writers. They see the structures of stories and borrow these for their own story writing. They find vocabulary in their reading that enriches their writing. They learn how to describe characters and places in a story and how to talk about what is significant in a plot. They learn how to present factual information, how to write captions for pictures, and how to inform their readers of the main idea. The books they read provide models for structure and style. Reading and writing are learned hand in hand, the one enriching the other. We cannot teach writing without providing the best possible examples of how to write.

And so we fill our classroom with books. In the next chapter we will look at book selection. Which books do we choose? What is good literature for children and how do we help students find the right book at the right time?

---

[6] Michele Landsberg, *Michele Landsberg's Guide to Children's Books* (Markham, Ontario: Penguin Books Canada, 1985), p. 194.

[7] Paul Hazard, *Books, Children and Men* (Boston: The Horn Book, 1944), p. 4.

Chapter 2

Choosing Books for the Classroom

"No book is really worth reading at the age of ten which is not equally (and often far more) worth reading at the age of fifty."

C. S. Lewis [8]

Which Book for Which Child ?

We might argue that a good book for a five-year-old also has a timeless appeal which means that both adults and children can enjoy it. What makes a good book for children? How can we select books for our classrooms that will meet the various needs of our young readers? When we open our classrooms to the world of children's books, how can we know that the books will be appropriate for the age of the children and their stage of reading development?

We need to seek a quality and an integrity in the writing and the illustrations which are lasting. This is why the Care Bears books, written by a computer, can never be more than transitory experiences. Children outgrow them because they offer nothing of substance. There is no writer to communicate with them.

Recently, a Grade 8 student told me that when she was little she had hated the monsters in *Where the Wild Things Are.* After a session in which we had been responding to picture books and discovering some of the many motifs in that book, she said that she now saw it differently. She was intrigued by Sendak's exploration of the boy's subconscious mind. She thought that the pictures had probably scared her as a child because she had fears which she couldn't identify but which might be manifest as monsters. Books such as this one have

[8] C. S. Lewis, "The Reader and All Kinds of Stories," *The Cool Web: The Pattern of Children's Reading,* ed. Margaret Meek et al. (London: The Bodley Head, 1977), p. 85.

many layers, which we peel away like the skin of an onion to reach the significance of the book for us. Each time we return to it at a different stage in life, we see new meanings.

Often adults respond to a stratum of meaning which is not recognized by the young children who enjoy the book for other reasons. *Peepo!* by Janet and Allan Ahlberg is full of visual treats for child readers as they follow the day of a baby and see the world through his eyes. For the adult reader, the nostalgic illustrations are evocative of times gone by; wartime Britain is the setting for the story. And the everyday happenings of the family emphasize the continuity of family life and some of its humor. Robert Munsch, speaking of his stories ***The Paper Bag Princess*** and ***Love You Forever,*** has called this dual appeal "bimodality." In the best children's books there is a little something for the adult reader to appreciate.

When selecting books for children, however, we must take care that adult tastes do not predominate. Children often love to read material about which we may feel less than enthusiastic. There is a time when they do love the Care Bears. We must be careful of being critical of the books children choose. We must learn to find what it is in those books that appeals to them so that we may guide their reading toward other books that will also satisfy but perhaps be more challenging in the ideas they present.

Conversely, we must not expect children to enjoy books just because we do. Many picture books now available are written for increasingly sophisticated audiences. Both illustrations and subject matter can be aimed at an adult audience and are best used in later grades. If you find yourself reading a book that is too sophisticated for young children, they will let you know. When you start to lose your audience it is a sure sign that the story is not holding their attention. Learning how to abandon a book is one of the reading skills we want to foster. Asking the class, "What do you think so far?" will often lead to honest responses that will suggest that you abandon a story. Be straightforward with the class. Sometimes we say, "Really, I'm not enjoying reading this to you. Do you mind if I stop?"

Four Things to Look for

Four criteria are important when selecting books for a primary classroom program.

1. *Content:* What is the book about?
2. *Language:* How is the content expressed?
3. *Attractiveness:* Does this book look and feel attractive?
4. *Ease of reading:* What is the difficulty and legibility of the text?

Content

Young children have a fundamental need to hear the world represented in story. In fact it is a right of childhood, a developmental necessity. Our collection of books will be first and foremost a collection of stories: traditional tales, folk and fairy stories, legends, myths, and wonder tales. It will include stories written by contemporary authors who use traditional formulas, repetition, and accumulation: writers such as Robert Munsch and Pat Hutchins.

There must also be books that are relevant to the children who read them; ones that reflect a world familiar to the child and present ideas and experiences at an age-appropriate level. Books provide a safe framework in which children can explore some of their psychological needs. All of us inevitably face change, trouble, loss, and uncertainty. These and many other emotional issues may be confronted and dealt with in books. One of the most important functions of literature for children is to reassure them that they are not alone in feeling as they do. Such concepts may be part of stories which have fantasy settings. ***Peter Rabbit***, for example, is the archetyepal naughty boy who must suffer the consequences of his disobedience while his good little brothers and sisters eat bread, milk, and blackberries. ***Curious George*** is another favorite. The naughty monkey who is too inquisitive has delighted children for generations. In my class the children began to call anyone who asked a lot of questions Curious George!

Other books show contemporary settings and children of all races and colors engaged in everyday activities. Ezra Jack Keats was one of the first artists and writers to show us black children in urban settings. *The Snowy Day* is a classic picture book about a small boy's pleasure in the snow, to which all children can relate. It is important to provide a balance between the real and the imaginary, the urban and the rural, the past and the present. Our children need to see themselves as they are, as well as in metaphors. Gary was a Nigerian boy newly arrived in our community. His face lit up with smiles when we read Sarah Hayes's and Jan Ormerod's *Eat Up, Gemma.* The brother who solves Gemma's eating problem looked exactly like Gary.

The content of children's books must be free from racial and sexual stereotyping and bias. Overt racism and sexism is often easy to spot. It is less obvious when it is implied by exclusions or by omission; for example, when books depict characters only in certain roles. The collection of books we use must contain stories and illustrations which show all people behaving in positive ways and in urban, twentieth-century settings. If we have bilingual children in our class we also seek out books in their language or find dual text editions. We show that we respect the cultural background of our children by the presence of these books in our collection.

Language

The language of the book is important in two ways. First, it is through the words of the text that children come to experience "writerly" ways of expression. Margaret Meek writes that: "The most important single lesson that children learn from texts is the nature and variety of written discourse, the different ways that language lets a writer tell, and the many and different ways a reader reads."[9]

Consider again the opening sentence of *The Very Hungry Caterpillar:* "In the light of the moon a little egg lay on a leaf." Most people would *tell* that information in a different way. The writer shines new light on an ordinary event. He fills a simple description with possibilities.

The language of storytellers is filled with rhythm and rhyme, metaphor and simile. Our first encounter with these forms of written language is in the literature that is used in children's books. The richness of words should never be diminished by

[9] Margaret Meek, *How Texts Teach What Readers Learn* (Stroud, Gloucester: The Thimble Press, 1988).

attempts to simplify text for beginning readers.

Secondly, the language of the text is important because it introduces new vocabulary to children and links those words to concepts that may be outside the child's actual experience. This way, their knowledge of the world and the words that refer to that knowledge is increased and their vocabulary grows. During a visit to the Caribbean, Anthony saw panniers on a donkey and said, "Oh, that's real. I thought it was only in books." Children's views of reality and fantasy are shaped by the stories they are read and told. Young children are still sorting out whether or not there really are slippers made of glass, carpets that fly, and donkeys that carry panniers. The more books they read the more they come to know.

Attractiveness

Books for young children are more attractive than ever as a result of changes in printing technology and the large number of artists and writers now working in the picture-book genre. Books for children should be attractive to look at and to handle. There is no need for us to have torn or broken books in our classrooms. Paperback books can be reinforced by covering them with clear plastic, which extends their life span by several years. Budget to replace worn paperbacks can be obtained when we consider these resources as essential and an alternative to workbooks. A classroom rich in literature has no need of drills and phonic exercises, and money formerly spent on these can be used to buy books.

The pictures are an important part of a first reading book, not only because illustrations embellish text but also because they provide contextual clues which assist the reader in decoding. The books that we choose for our classrooms should represent a variety of artistic styles, ranging from the simplicity and bright color of Lois Ehlert, Tomie de Paola, and Dick Bruna to the detail and complexity of Brian Wildsmith, Susan Jeffers, and Steven Kellog. Books illustrated by photographs offer another sort of artistic experience; readers of all ages appreciate Tana Hoban's beautiful concept books. The books now available offer exquisite examples of water-color, pastel, collage, and pen-and-ink techniques and can be incorporated into the art curriculum as well.

Wordless picture books like those of John Goodall tell a story entirely in illustrations. They demand much of the reader and are a good introduction to the active role of the reader in constructing text.

Sometimes the story told in the pictures and the story told in the words are totally dependent upon each other. In Pat Hutchins's **One Hunter** we see hidden in the bush the animals of which the hunter is oblivious until the last page. Text and illustrations both tell the story. The children see what is happening and what will happen, and can hardly contain their excitement as the number of animals grows.

In the school library resource centre, we can find a wide range of enormously attractive hardcover picture books to complement the paperbacks used in the classroom. Children should have a daily opportunity to visit the library to select books for their personal reading and for use in the classroom. Careful planning of purchases by teachers and teacher-librarians can ensure that the resources in a school are complementary. Together they can plan for author studies, theme units, and the blending of fiction and nonfiction titles to explore ideas.

Ease of Reading

Trade books are designed and printed in a wide variety of sizes, shapes, fonts, and formats. The ease or difficulty of a book for a child reader derives from the complex interaction between several factors. The textual features of books that contribute to readability include:

- size of print;
- number of words on a page;
- number of words in a sentence;
- where line breaks occur (at the end of a clause makes for easier reading); and
- the match between the words and the pictures (is the meaning obvious?).

The features of language that contribute to the readability include:

- language patterns; i.e., syntactic predictability ;
- repetition of sentences;
- repetition of refrains;

- rhyming words;
- words from children's oral language;
- words that repeat frequently;
- words and sentences that are predictable from pictures;
- story structures that drive the reader to the conclusion; and
- stories that are personally relevant to the reader.

These readability features of language and print are found in combination in all books. We must provide a wide range of books to meet the needs of readers at all stages of their reading development, from the prereader who cannot yet make a match between symbol and sound, to the fluent reader who is beginning to develop stamina and to tackle first novels.

Children at all stages of fluency are found in all grades in our regular primary classrooms. It is the nature of reading development that it does not happen simultaneously for all the children in a class at any given moment. We have taught Grade 1 children who read novels, Grade 2 children who are still in need of linguistically supportive pattern books, and Grade 3 children who have just cracked the code and are beginning to read independently. There is a continuum of development, but children move along it at different rates. We expect independence to be achieved by the latter part of Grade 2, but we know that it can come much earlier, and that for a few children we will need to offer extra support for a longer period of time.

From our experience with child readers at all levels of fluency and skill, we have developed a list of good books which meet all the above criteria and provide an excellent core of material for a literature-rich classroom language program.

The *Real Books for Reading* Bibliography: How to Use It

Real books in primary classroom programs are used in many different ways and for many different purposes. Some of these include:

- teacher reading aloud to the class;
- children spending time reading by themselves;
- children sharing a book with a partner;

- children reading aloud to the teacher;
- children reading aloud to an older buddy;
- children reading at home to a parent or sibling;
- parents reading aloud to children at home;
- other adults or older buddies reading aloud at school;
- children reading books to research information;
- children reading books to compare versions;
- children reading books to study the work of one author;
- children reading books on which to model their own stories; and
- children listening to tape-recorded stories.

For all these purposes we use the same books. It is important that the children see the same books often and in all the reading situations that occur both at school and at home. Therefore we need a wide range of books, and these books need to be organized. Because one of the key components of the program is the child's experience of reading aloud to the teacher, we want to be able to find books quickly for that purpose. Consequently, we sort the books not by theme but by categories that reflect the stages of reading development through which all children pass. Another significant aspect of the program is the sharing of books at home. When children practise their emerging reading skills at home, it must be with stories that they can read successfully. Again, we need to be able to find books at a certain level quickly.

We have found, by consulting with children in the primary grades and by taking the features of texts into account, that we can group books into a number of categories according to the textual demands that they make upon the reader. The children help us to compile a collection of books that match their own level of reading independence. They sort and debate putting together books that they can read easily. When the sorting is complete, the children find that if they can read one book in a category – say, *Coco Can't Wait* – then it is highly probable that they can read the other books grouped in that category, such as *Just Like Daddy*, *A Dark Dark Tale*, and *Whose Mouse Are You?* Using this system, the children can be sure to find a wide selection of books available at their reading level that cover all sorts of topics and ideas.

As we group the books, we look at the dominant features of

each category and write descriptions that help us to assign a place to new acquisitions.

As we acquire new books for the collection, we decide together the category into which each must be placed. All books are color-coded so that they can be easily located and replaced after use. Sturdy plastic tool caddies are excellent for storing books and for carrying them to different places in the classroom.

In talking about stages we must make it absolutely clear that we do **not** see each stage as discrete. Children's language learning is never linear. Sometimes there is regression to a previous stage to practise familiar skills and experience complete control. Sometimes there are leaps ahead, especially when purpose drives the learning. We have seen early readers struggle with difficult text because they really want to find out about dinosaurs or some other important topic. When we think of a child as being at a particular stage, it is because they are comfortable and confident independent readers with that material. A beginning reader is independent with a concept or wordless picture book but will read a story like **The Paper Bag Princess** by telling about the pictures.

Another problem we have in talking about stages is that teachers may feel that students should work only with material appropriate to their particular stage of growth. Any system which codes books according to reading level runs into the problem of competitiveness among children and the implication that children at a higher level are superior to those at a lower level. On the contrary, working with literature should mean that children will read widely, as they do at home, from books at all levels of difficulty. The joy of using real books is that we do not restrict the children to one grade-appropriate set of readers. The content of the book is what is important to the child reader, not the reading level. When a wide range of material is available, children move back and forth between the books, sometimes reading the words, sometimes reading only the key words, sometimes reading only the pictures. They will choose very wisely to practise their independent reading skills with books that offer them the least difficulty, but they will enjoy looking at pictures in books at all levels.

We have learned that a successful reading experience for young children, when they try to read independently, is the result of an interaction between their determination to read *this* book, on *this* occasion; the skills and strategies for decoding that they bring to this endeavor; and the demands of the text itself. What we are trying to do as teachers is help make the most effective match that we can between the reading abilities of the students and the demands that are made upon them by the text. When a child brings a book to us, or takes a book home to read to a parent, we want the child to experience as much success and as little frustration as possible. The organization of the books into stages allows us to help children find a number of books that are all more or less similar in terms of their textual difficulty.

Finally, a word about ages and grades. We expect our children to develop as readers in kindergarten, Grade 1, and Grade 2. Most will be independent by late Grade 2. Some will come to Grade 1 already reading. The whole point of a program that uses real books is that it gives us the flexibility to meet the individual needs of the children in the class, whatever their ages and abilities. The children we are describing in this book are in kindergarten, Grade 1 and Grade 2 classrooms. The ways in which we respond to them in the reading situation depends upon *what they can do* and therefore *what they need to know next* to develop as enthusiastic readers. The program is the same whatever the grade. The difference between a Grade 2 and a kindergarten class lies, of course, in the number of fluent independent readers, the types of books they read and are read, and the volume and depth of the written responses that we expect from the children.

Chapter **3**

Stages of Reading Development and Real Books for Reading

The Five Stages of Reading Development

The observant teacher will see milestones in the child's development as a reader. We have identified five stages which we think are descriptive of the normal child's developmental progress in the primary years. Though the speed with which children pass through these stages varies, it is generally the case that there is a common progression through the stages. The categories into which the books are organized correspond to the stages **in that a child reading independently and aloud will experience success with these books.** Of course there are other ways in which children interact with books, and there is no intention on our part to suggest that children at a certain stage should read only those books that they can read alone. Rather the opposite; children should hear stories read aloud that are too difficult for them to read, and they should choose easier text when they are reading to a younger child or practising reading with an adult.

Stage One: The Prereader

These are our very youngest children who have had the least experience with reading. The children at this stage do not realize that the words on the page correspond to the talk that comes from a reader's lips. They tell stories with great gusto and read pictures, but they do not have concepts about print. These children may not know the meaning of the words that we use when we refer to print, such as *letter, sound,* and *sentence.* When they bring a book to share with the teacher, it is the adult who will do the reading. The child will chime in with predictable parts or predict words at the ends of sentences. When they write, these children experiment with letters and sounds and may represent words with symbols other than letters.

Playing at being a waiter, Arden wrote out the order he took in the pizza parlor:

When these children come to share books with us we choose from the following categories:

Concept Books

These books have one word or a very short phrase and a picture. The words and picture match perfectly. Usually these books simply label a concept or an object. Alphabet books and counting books fall into this category. Jan Pienkowski has written and illustrated a visually appealing series that names

Colors, Homes, and *Time* among others. Such books can be used as first dictionaries by children at a later stage. Very occasionally we find a book in this category that also tells a story, such as Pat Hutchins's **One Hunter** and Byron Barton's **Where's Al?,** but in both of these books the narrative is contained in the pictures and not in the words. Using books such as these, nonreaders can experience instant success and begin to see the printed word as having a meaningful relationship with a picture.

Wordless Picture Books

Telling a story from pictures is part of reading, and practising with these books develops both story sense and book-handling skills. These books offer a chance to explore story structure and detail in illustrations.

John Goodall has a series of books in this category, and one of our favorites is **Up and Up** by Shirley Hughes. These books can also be used in increasingly sophisticated ways for drama and story writing.

Pattern Books

With their very strong rhythms and linguistic patterns, these books can also be used successfully with prereading children. Usually one sentence and one picture appear on a page, and only one word changes from page to page. These are the simplest of the pattern books, and many good examples of the type can be found in the early stages of reading schemes, e.g., Methuen Terraced House Books, Methuen Instant Readers, Ginn Story Box, and Nelson Early Birds. The most famous and perfect of all pattern books is **Brown Bear, Brown Bear, What Do You See?** by Bill Martin Jr. and Eric Carle. Prereading children become instantly familiar with the pattern and "read" the story with great gusto. They do not yet make an accurate sound-to- print match.

Poetry

Nursery rhymes and poems are extremely important reading for these children. They memorize rhymes and read them to themselves, and develop an ear for the rhythms and cadences of language. Poetry is a neglected literary form and few adults, even dedicated readers of fiction, will admit to reading poetry. The roots of a love of poetry begin with Mother Goose, and so traditional rhymes play a large part in the language program. Prereading children can collect their own favorite rhymes in a personal anthology and bring it to read to us.

Stage Two: The Beginning Reader

Children at this stage have realized that the print carries the meaning. Their alphabetic knowledge is developing, and in their writing they represent words with appropriate salient sounds. They are phonetic writers, basing their representations of letter sounds on what they hear and representing each syllable by one letter (e.g., WT for water, JGN for dragon), as shown in this drawing and commentary by Aileen:

When they read, they rely heavily on their previous experience with the book. They memorize patterns; and while they may look at the first letter of an unknown word, the concept of word-to-sound correspondence is still not fully established. Children at this stage still need concept books, pattern books, and poetry which they can read independently. Frequent repetition of the same text builds confidence, a feeling of success and a familiarity with the habit of reading, and helps develop awareness of the one-to-one correspondence of print to sound. Parents often say to us, "But they're only memorizing." Our reply is, "Yes, isn't it great that they've reached this stage. Now we are going to look at some simple stories together that will move them on to use more complex reading strategies."

First Steps

Books in this category have a picture and a sentence on every page. Sentence structures may be repeated throughout the book, or they may change from page to page as new information is introduced. The books have a simple story to tell and the vocabulary is easily predictable from the pictures. The print is relatively large and well spaced. Early-reading children can read these simple stories with the help of an adult or by themselves if it is not their first experience with the book. They will read the pictures, chime in with ends of sentences or with repetitions, and will learn how to turn pages and look for the printed word.

Pumpkin, Pumpkin by Jeanne Titherington is a wonderful example of this sort of book. The text is simple – a single sentence broken into clauses, each with its own soft, detailed illustration drawn with pencil crayons. On the first page is a picture of Jamie's hand holding a single pumpkin seed. He plants the seed and watches it grow. On the last page he shows us the six seeds he saves from his pumpkin for planting in the spring. The text is predictable and simple but the book is a delightful introduction for young children to the cycle of life and growth. Jamie is watched in his garden by many small creatures who are not mentioned in the text but who are part of the book nevertheless. We have enjoyed this book with many beginning readers who have found the rhythm of the language easy to read. This is a great book for Halloween or for springtime reading.

Stage Three: The Emergent Reader

Children at this stage have made a breakthrough. This is the stage at which they pester people constantly to hear them read. They know that each word is separate and corresponds to one spoken word. They can find isolated words on a page, point to first letters, and follow print accurately across the page. They read books they know with accuracy. They frequently finger point to keep their place and are developing a small sight vocabulary. They use picture clues and possibly initial consonants to help decode unknown words. When they write these children use vowels as well as consonants, though not always the accurate vowel. They spell using phonics, understanding that letters in combination make certain sounds. At this stage they may have introduced spacing into their writing. Jessie's description of her affection for turtles provides a good example of these emerging skills:

These children need to continue to read pattern and "First Steps" books to build confidence and demonstrate success. They are also able to tackle books from the next category, "Step a Little Further."

Step a Little Further

Books in this category are similar in structure to the "First Steps" books. They tell a story; they have print which is relatively well spaced; there is a picture and only one or two sentences on a page. The vocabulary and the concepts may be unusual or more difficult, but the language structures are close to the oral language patterns of young children, and the stories usually concern events that are familiar from a child's experience.

Some of the favorites in this category are *Just Like Daddy* by Frank Asch, *Across the Stream* by Mirra Ginsburg and Nancy Tafuri (notable for its lovely large print and the rhyming structure), and *How Do I Put It On?*, the first in the series by Shigeo Watanabe about a little bear. This last title is a book that is made easy to read by its syntactic structure. The story is told in the form of question and answer. "Do I put it on like this?" asks the bear with his cap on his foot. The children use the syntactic cuing system together with the picture to supply the answer. "No! I put my cap on my head."

Step a Little Faster

Books in this category have pictures which still provide most of the information needed to tell the story. The pictures help the reader predict specific vocabulary in the text. Help may also be available in the form of strong rhymes or rhythms or in the frequent repetition of an idea or phrase. These books are longer than those in the "Step a Little Further" section and more complex. There is more than one sentence on a page, the print may be smaller, and the vocabulary may be more difficult or unusual.

Children need a little more stamina to achieve independence with these books. One of our favorites is *Each Peach Pear Plum* by Janet and Allan Ahlberg. Each page introduces a new nursery rhyme or storybook character hidden in an unusual place. The children love to point out where they all are! The success they have with this book often leads them to try *The Jolly Postman,* even though the words in that book are much more difficult to read. The Ahlberg fans in the class will read the book and the letters it contains from story characters and will find all the intertextual references that the authors have deliberately included.

Stage Four: The Developing Reader

These children have "taken off" into reading. Sometimes it seems to happen overnight – they go home one day unable to read and come to school next day with a whole new outlook on the process! They use a combination of semantic, syntactic, and phonic cues to decode words they don't know. They have a developed sight vocabulary, and when they write they space their words and use vowels. Many words show their beginning mastery of conventional spelling, as Sarah's letter about bears demonstrates:

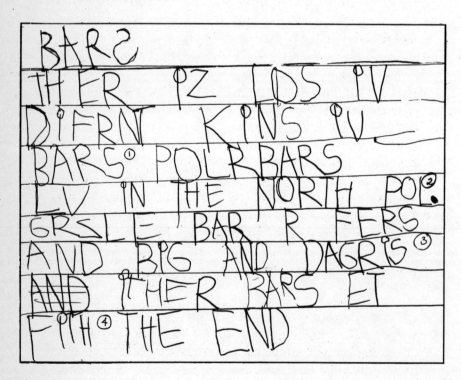

While these children know *how* to read, they lack the stamina needed for novels and still need the support of pictures, clearly printed text, and familiar vocabulary. They read most easily from books that have familiar content though they are able to attempt unfamiliar words. They may decode a word without knowing what it means. The following categories of books offer them a diverse choice of reading material.

Taking Off

Books in this category have considerably more print on a page. The print may be smaller or more closely spaced on the page, or may be presented in an unusual format. The syntactic patterns may be beginning to move away from everyday structures and to take on the more formal properties of written language. *Peepo!*, again by the Ahlbergs, *Mister Magnolia* by Quentin Blake, *Frog and Toad Are Friends* by Arnold Lobel, and *Peace at Last* by Jill Murray are books that can now be read fluently. Remember, though, that all these books have been enjoyed at previous stages. *Peepo!* is a wonderful book to share with prereaders, because they read "Peepo!" every time it appears, while you read the rest of the text.

You're Away

Books in this category still have a picture on every page, but there is more text and the print is smaller. The stories are longer and the literary quality of the language is more apparent. Many books at this stage begin to address issues that may be important to young children and there is less assistance for the reader from rhyme or repetition. Some favorite books in this category are *Gorilla* by Anthony Browne, a story about a lonely little girl's relationship with her father, *Corduroy* by Don Freeman, and *The Snowy Day* by Ezra Jack Keats.

Stage Five: The Independent Reader

Children at this stage can read well. They have developed some stamina and can now read silently. They are developing the habit of reading and can talk about the books they have read. They begin to read longer books and first novels. As writers, these children use standard spelling except when tackling a long, difficult word.

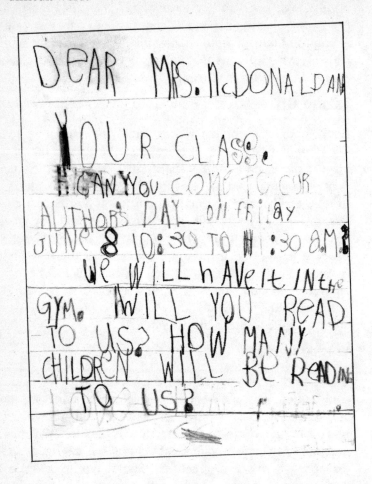

There are many picture books that are suitable in content and style for these children, as well as books that look more like novels. The books in the next categories help children make the transition from picture books to first novels and lead the newly independent reader into the world of full-length books.

On Your Own at Last

At this stage the pictures have become less important for predicting text, although the amount of print is made more easily digestible by the presence of pictures on every page. The print is not large and the style of writing is increasingly literary, with written forms taking precedence over oral. Many books at this stage resemble novels in appearance if not in length or in the stamina required of the reader. Most do not have chapters and can still be read in one sitting.

Getting Longer

These stories require some stamina on the part of the reader. Not only is there more print on a page, but the stories are longer and more complex. The vocabulary is more sophisticated; however, most of these books still make the print digestible by having a picture on every page and by focusing on thoughts and themes familiar to young children. This category includes some of the more challenging picture books as well as some that have the format of novels.

First Novels

This category continues to make demands on the reader in terms of the length of the books, the size and quantity of print on a page, and the thought-provoking nature of the content. The author's message is carried primarily by the text, although there may be a few well-placed illustrations to break the density of the print. Most of these books feature chapters or a collection of short stories. It takes more than a single reading to finish one of these books.

As well as housing this range of fiction, a well-equipped primary classroom will have other reading material available for different purposes. The following materials should be represented:
- audio-visual materials, including books and tapes;
- children's own published writing;
- reference books;
- dictionaries and encyclopedias;
- maps and atlases;
- puzzle and quiz books;
- magazines, comics, catalogues, and newspapers;
- posters, labels, and notices; and
- greetings cards.

Given all these resources, the next question to be addressed is how to use them. What do we do when we are listening to children read at their different growth points? How do we use a book with a beginning reader and how do we use the same book with a fluent reader? How do we organize the classroom so that young children may have the maximum opportunity to engage in genuine acts of reading and writing? How do we teach reading and writing using real books?

Chapter 4

Sharing Books With Children

The Reading Conference

We are convinced, both by experience and research, that the more frequently young children read and listen to stories individually with a caring adult, the more easily they become independent readers and writers. It is crucial to the success of the program that we make the time to share books with individuals on a regular basis. In the course of these reading conferences we can :

- ensure that we offer the child the right support at the right time, modifying the responses we make so that the child gains the most from the experience;
- suggest strategies for tackling unknown words;
- encourage the child to keep on reading and help boost morale;
- keep track of reading progress;
- model ways of talking about books and writers; and
- suggest further reading experiences.

The teacher's listening and sharing time is of course severely rationed because of the number of children in the class. Thus it is crucial that this time be used to best advantage. While we share books with individual children, the rest of the class must be busy with other tasks that do not need our constant intervention, such as writing, creating, building, or sharing a book with a friend.

If a child is interested in a book, the task of reading to an adult is not only less threatening but also more successful and hence enjoyable. Therefore we always begin this special sharing time with the statement, "Find a book that you would like to share with me." We have a wide selection of books available, touching on many different areas of interest from which each reader can make his or her selection. How we share the book they choose changes, of course, from one child to the next. We *modify* our instructional listening and sharing to suit each individual child's level of reading skill. Children read books in a number of ways. Each requires different responses from the professional listener.

When we are sharing a book with a child, we use their **reading log** to record our observations about their knowledge of print. The reading log is a scribbler or notebook ruled up in three columns.

This is Peter's seventh reading log, from February of his Grade 1 year.

Reading Log # 7 Peter		
title	Date	Comment
Where the wild Things Are;	Jan 29	– retells me story – memorized very animated / accurate – beginning to look at pictures – Buddy read / Have you seen my duck!
Babys Catalogue	Jan 30	☺
I Can Do it	Feb 1	shared time – I read most at first – gets idea – fills in appropriately
Reading	Feb 2	– together – easy – suggest read together / I like books
I like Books	Feb 6.	☺ ☺
Things I like	Feb 7	reads alone – first brings it to me – reads it – break thru / – Island My Tale
Cat on the Mat	Feb 8	easy read . suggest
Mother Mother I want another	Feb 13 another	fills in appropriately shared – reads much of it – tires – – alone.
Coco Can't Wait	Feb 16	☺ good – substitutes with meaning . read 75% break through . fluent / few errors
Fix–It	Feb 20	shared
Meg and Mog	Feb 26	hard read – difficult set up of other books text ... / suggest

There is a space to record the title and the date of the reading. There is also a space for a comment. This log is a record of everything that Peter reads in the classroom.

In the first entry he filled in the title and the date of the reading by himself. I used the comment section to note that he has retold the story with gusto and total accuracy. I also made myself a note to suggest to his buddy reader (see chapter six) that they share the pattern book *Have You Seen My Duckling?* by Nancy Tafuri at their next visit.

The next entry was done independently by Peter after one of his frequent visits to the library corner. He carefully filled in the comment section with a happy face to tell us he liked the book. The third entry is again a record of a reading time that Peter and I spent together. I used the comment section to note that during this time I read some of the text and Peter filled in where he could.

This log is a very important record-keeping device for me. It allows me to keep track of what Peter is reading and how often he is reading with me. It also allows me to suggest further independent reading material to him. I give Peter Anthony Browne's *Things I Like* to read during the next work-period time. I find that when I follow up on these suggestions, the children are more eager to extend their reading selections and venture into new territory!

This personal reading log is also used by Peter himself, as it is by other children who are beginning and developing readers, to record what they have read independently during the individual or book-corner reading time. This information is very valuable to me in our reading conferences. I can see if Peter has read a particular story before, if it is one of a series of stories that he enjoys, or if it is a first-time read. This information helps me modify my responses so that the help I offer is of the utmost value.

Reading With the Prereading Child

Timothy is a lively four-year-old who loves to pore over books. He spends many profitable hours in the library corner with his friends and stuffed animals reading from memory his favorite tales and poems. He delights in the pictures, the rhythm of the language, and his ability to entertain. He often brings his favorite book, **Mister Magnolia**, to read to me. For children such as Timothy who are at this stage, a reading session is simply a matter of having an adult listen to them retell an often-heard story and confirm their skill at this task. Children who read in this manner often select old favorites such as **Each Peach Pear Plum**; **Rosie's Walk**; **Where the Wild Things Are**; and **Jillian Jiggs**. For these children we spend our instructional time talking about their choice of book and sharing the humor, pathos, or information that this book offers. We draw the children's attention to the pictures and encourage them to extend the text of the story using the information found in the illustrations. Toward the end of the session we might read a short pattern or concept book that we think the child could easily begin to read independently, inviting them to notice the print on the page. With Timothy I read books such as **What a Tale**, **Where's Spot?**, and **Home Sweet Home. Where's Spot?** was our all-time favorite as Timothy tried to guess what was under each flap. We close this time together by helping Timothy and children like him to fill in their reading log with the titles of the books we have shared.

Reading With the Beginning Reader

These readers are already independently reading the same pattern books that we are sharing with the prereading child. When Yusef, a beginning reader, brings me the pattern book **Cat on the Mat** by Brian Wildsmith, my responses are different from those I give to Timothy when he is simply retelling a favorite story.

All I need to do is set the initial pattern and Yusef is successfully and proudly able to complete the story. I begin the reading with "The cat sat on the..." and pause on the word "mat." I wait for Yusef to guess. He immediately fills in with the word "mat." Then together we examine the next page and try to guess who will sit on the mat next. Yusef looks carefully at the pictures and identifies the picture of the dog. He reads with me, "The dog sat on the mat..." Now he has the pattern and the idea that the pictures will clue him to the print. Together we turn the pages, examine the pictures, and predict the text, and *he* finishes the reading independently. With beginning readers such as

Yusef, we consciously teach our students the strategy of using picture and contextual clues to make logical predictions about the words. We continually stress that print holds meaning. We introduce these readers to books from the category "First Steps." Some special favorites are John Burningham's *The Snow, The School*, and *The Dog,* among others; Jeanne Titherington's *Pumpkin, Pumpkin*; and some of the Shigeo Watanabe books such as *How Do I Eat It?* and *Hello, How Are You*?

Sometimes a beginning reader like six-year-old Gus brings a book such as *Coco Can't Wait* that is slightly too hard for him to read independently. When he immediately begins to stumble on the beginning words "Coco lives on the top of the hill," we know that a different response is required. We must do more of the reading. We begin the text, "Coco lives on the top of the..." and pause at the word "hill" (we usually select a noun or an action word to pause on) to encourage Gus to carry on the reading. Then we pick up the text at "in the" and "with the." We read only what he cannot read – usually the function words. Remember these little function words are largely redundant to the meaning.

A question we must decide is when to pick up the reading. How long is too long to wait? A successful strategy is to give a silent count of five before telling the reader the troublesome word or group of words. We correct the child's own reading only if it alters the meaning of the text drastically. In *Coco Can't Wait,* Gus substitutes "grandmother" for "grandma." We make *no* comment about this kind of error.

On completion of this sharing time, we usually suggest simple pattern books that these readers can read independently with a friend, a parent volunteer, their reading buddy, or with their parents and/or siblings at home. A good suggestion is the Brian Wildsmith pattern book, *What a Tale*, or his "First Steps" book, *The Island.* We record these suggestions along with the stories we have shared in the child's personal reading log.

This is an exciting stage for both of us as the child's progress is often rapid. Gus moved from reading very simple pattern books to "First Steps" books in a matter of weeks. As he gained skill through practice and repeated success, less and less help was required from me. We have found that, at this particular stage of reading development, teachers are the child's best listeners because of our skill in knowing when to pause, when to fill in words, and when to correct the child's efforts. Thus we try, if possible, to see these children every day for a few minutes to read, read, read.

Reading With the Emergent Reader

When Alyssa comes to read with me I know from other reading sessions that she can read with word-to-sound correspondence. She reads the print rather than the pictures. Two areas of difficulty that readers like Alyssa encounter are stopping when they meet an unfamiliar word, or reading a word inaccurately and changing the meaning of the sentence. When Alyssa stops on the word "tucked" in Maria Polushkin's story *Mother, Mother, I Want Another* and looks to me for help, I suggest she leave out the problem word and keep on reading. When she finishes the page we go back to figure out the word. She is able to use the semantic cuing system to do this. There are a number of other strategies that we use to get children like Alyssa moving forward again. We suggest that the reader:

- start again and reread the sentence;
- consider possible meanings for the word: What makes sense here?
- look at the first letter: What sound does that make? Maybe that will give you a clue.

While we are deliberately teaching the children to use semantic, syntactic, and phonic cues we *do not* belabor this. As soon as the mechanical process of reading starts taking over the joy, the desire to read is lost.

When Alyssa reads a harder book for her, Thacher Hurd's *Mama Don't Allow,* and miscues "The Swamp Band played far into the lake" instead of "The Swamp Band played far into the night," she has changed the meaning of the story. I stop her and ask if what she read made sense to her. When she replies, "Not really," I direct her to reread the sentence and look carefully at the last word. She immediately says, "That isn't right. It doesn't start like lake." With some help from me she is able to figure out that the word is "night," not "lake." When I now ask her if this makes sense, she says, "Of course, it starts and ends right..."

When children read a word inaccurately and change the meaning, we must continually pose the question, "Does that make sense to you?" If the children respond in the negative or seem unsure, we tell them to make another guess until the text makes sense to them. If their miscues or errors make sense, we do not correct them. But at the end of the reading time we *may* go back and examine some of these words. At this point we suggest that the children use their knowledge of phonics to make another guess. We are very selective about using this technique; if overused, it can undermine the fragile confidence of the children.

At the end of the sharing time, we ask the children to fill in their reading logs, and take the opportunity to suggest other text they could read independently. I suggest to Alyssa, who seems to like funny books, that she read Peter Goodspeed's *A Rhinoceros Wakes Me Up in the Morning.* The books we might suggest are from the categories "Step a Little Further" and "Step a Little Faster." We also try to link these suggestions to current classroom interests. I suggest to Alyssa that she read *The Last Puppy* by Frank Asch, as the class has just begun a unit on pets.

Reading With Developing and Independent Readers

When we listen to children who read fluently, self-correct their errors, and understand the author's meaning, we know the battle of cracking the code has been won! It is no longer necessary for us to hear them read every word of the story. They are able to decode the text by themselves, but they still require our help to probe the deeper meanings of the story. After Jeremy read Charlotte Zolotow's *My Grandson Lew,* he and I shared together the pain of the death of our grandfathers. Jeremy remembered how his grandfather, even when he was sick, played card games with him. I told him about the mock World War I battles, complete with toy horses and riders, that my grandfather and I used to enact in my grandmother's back vegetable patch. We both cried. I gave him Susan Varley's book *Badger's Parting Gifts* and told him that it had made me feel a little better about death. After reading the book he said, "It's a good book but not as good as *Wilfrid Gordon McDonald Partridge*. It helps you think of really good memories."

It is with newly fluent children like Jeremy that we use a *reading response journal*. We want to establish a dialogue between us, reader to reader, equal in our enjoyment of books. We want the children to explore the kinds of feelings that stories evoke in us as readers. A reading response journal makes the connection between reading and writing, provides us with a record of the reading conference and the books that we have shared, and gives us insights into the understandings that children have brought to their reading. We have no need to set comprehension questions, because what the children write in their journals shows us what they have understood. They, not the teacher, set the agenda. They show us what was significant for them in the story. It is our responsibility to respond to the child's ideas and to extend the learning.

Each child has a notebook in which, when they have finished reading a story independently, they record the title of the book, the date read, and a short comment. We encourage the children to write a letter to us, not retelling every detail of the story but rather expressing what feelings this story evoked and what links to their own lives were illuminated. This letter provides a starting point for our reading conference. It gives us an entrance into the children's thoughts and feelings. At the conclusion of the reading conference, we take the time to reply in letter form. We offer some glimpse into our own lives and the ways that books have touched us. We usually end our reply with a comment that requires some response from the child. In this way a dialogue is established over time. When we show this kind of interest, the children's responses are richer and more insightful.

One day Alison brought a new copy of Robin Muller's *Tatterhood* to school and I read it at read-aloud time to the class. This led to much discussion about heroines in stories. In Alison's reading response journal I pose the question, "Do you know any other books with brave girls in them?" Here is her reply and the written conversation that ensued over the next few days:

Dear Alison, I love the book you brought.
Tarrerhood is very brave. Do you know
any other books with brave girls in them?

love from Ms. Wells, Sept. 16th

Dear Ms Wells I Dono tgirl That is Brave
Mollie WHuppIE and The Giant her
sistrs wer shardt And Mollie whuppie
Want a crossl Litte Bit of hair
carring A sistr at a time
Mollie whuppie Was Brave
Veroy verey Brave. From alison

Dear Alison, Please read Do Not Open.
Do you think Miss Moodie is brave?

Dear MS We Ells.   love from Ms wells

miss Moodie is brave verey verey
Brave BuT She is
Skand Of Mes
From Alison

Dear Alison,
William gets scared too so
he has a tiny little light that stays on all night.
Read 'There's a Nightmare in my Closet' by
Mercer Mayer. What does the boy do in that story?

love from Ms W.

Dear Ms. W.

The NIGhTMARE iN my
CLOSET. Was NoT SkARy
At All AND The little

Boy Was MaD But
Not To MaD He WoD Not
peek arand to look Be hend
hem cose he was To

Skard to look Love
From alison

Dear Alison,
The Amazing Bone is about a pig called Pearl. Is she brave? Tell me what happens to her.
love from Ms Wells

Dear misswells.
pearl is not Brave not
One Bit Brave. She Was
skard When The Bone Torki
She Was skard of The fox Alot.
Love From Alison

Dear Alison,
What does Meg do when she is scared of the ghost?
love, Ms.W.

Dear ms.W.
She maks a spell

Do you ever get scared of anything Ali?
When I go To Bed cose
IT is so DrKE.

On another occasion a class wrote to their teacher after she had read **Leo the Late Bloomer** to them. The authors thank Jane Murphy and her students in the O. M. MacKillop Public School for sharing the following samples of their work:

Jennifer
Leo the Late Bloomer reminds me of my mom told me of when my cousin didn't talk until she was three years old.Mrs. M. what does the story remind you of ?

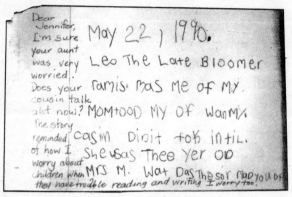

Jason
Leo the Late Bloomer
It reminded me of when I didn't know how to spell
and then a few minutes later I spelled a word finally.

> May 22, 1990.
> Leo the late Bloomer
> It remindid me of
> wan I didn now how
> to spaell and than a
> few minit lader I spaelld
> a werod finle.

Carmen
Leo the Late Bloomer
The book about Leo the Late Bloomer it reminded me of when
I was a baby. My mom worried about me because I had no hair.
But now I have hair.

Chris
Leo the Late Bloomer
It reminded me of when I couldn't read and write
even on paper but I could say a word.

Sharing time with children who can read is not so much a matter of listening to them as they practise decoding, but more a matter of helping them respond to the stories to deepen their comprehension.

It has also been our experience that fluent young readers, like their adult counterparts, read books that require varying degrees of reading skills. Seven-year-old Robert is a fluent reader in Grade 1. His reading log shows that he read an old favorite, *Fix-It,* one day; began the first novel *Flat Stanley* the next day; and then turned to a McDonald Starter's book on *Snakes*.

Interest, availability, peer recommendations, and the mood of the time all play a part in what the children select to read, just as they do for adults. We encourage this way of selecting reading materials and only intervene when the children seem to be in a reading rut, afraid to branch out into new and different genres. The record of titles read is of great importance because it gives us information about what the children have been reading and if it is necessary to intervene in their choices.

We use many different strategies to lure these readers toward new and more challenging texts.

- We read a book to the class and then suggest the child read another book by the same author.
- We keep a collection of books that the children have recommended as "must reads" on permanent display in the classroom.
- We regularly collect books by one special author,

research the author's background, and make a display to be shared by the whole class. We can direct hesitant readers to this collection.

• As part of our theme centre, we always have many different books at different levels of difficulty to be pored over by the children. We might suggest that the child who is in a reading rut research the theme, using the books available as a starting point.

This approach to teaching reading allows us to work with children with widely different reading abilities who are interested in the same book. Literature, unlike some basals, lends itself beautifully to use by children with different reading skills. A book such as ***Mr. Gumpy's Outing*** can be retold by Timothy, a prereader, partially read by Gus, a beginning reader, and fluently enjoyed by Alyssa, a developing reader. It is up to us as professional listeners to modify our responses so that each of these readings is both successful and productive for the child.

For Timothy, who retells me an old favorite, I enjoy the rendition, praise his skill, laugh with him at the pictures, and ask him to tell me who he thinks made the boat tip. He looks at me with concentration and says, "I don't think it was any one person, it was them all. What do you think?" Talk is generated by this reading and our time is spent sharing our ideas. Gus needs me to share the reading with him. My role is to put in the function words and any other vocabulary that he finds difficult so that the flow of the reading is not inhibited or interrupted. Alyssa fluently decodes this text, self-corrects her errors, and understands the author's meaning. However, she tires before the ending of the book and I finish the reading. Alison reads this book to the end by herself. She requires a response from me that will deepen her understanding of the text and help her to place this story into the context of her own life. I ask her to think what she would do if she was tipped out of a boat. She responds very quickly, "I'll be okay, I always wear a life jacket. I have a boat and a cottage. I know all about boats, my dad and mom taught me." The more we work with real books, the more we realize how these books can serve a variety of purposes for different readers.

Teachers often ask us, But how do you know what kind of

responses to make to children? How do you know when to take over the reading? How do you know when to correct? The answer to all these questions is quite simple. LISTEN TO THE CHILDREN READ, TAKE INTO ACCOUNT THE CHILD'S STAGE OF READING DEVELOPMENT, AND THEN USE YOUR COMMON SENSE. Remember to view errors not as dreadful mistakes but as windows to more effective instruction. Listening to children read is the key component of our language program.

It is also important to EXAMINE THE CHILDREN'S WRITING.

Children such as Allan who are still experimenting with letters and sounds and have not yet established a clear sound/letter understanding are usually at the memorization stage of the reading process. They are the prereaders.

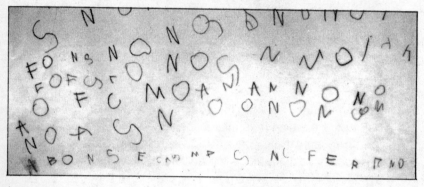

Anthi has the beginnings of an understanding of how words are constructed and represents words with one or more dominant sounds.

Remember, children like Anthi can usually read, with a little pattern setting by the teacher, simple pattern and "First Steps" books. These are the beginning readers.

Joel's emerging skill in composition is shown by his use of spaces, conventional spellings for the more common function words (is, and, the) and by his ability to identify correctly, for the most part, the dominant sounds in individual words.

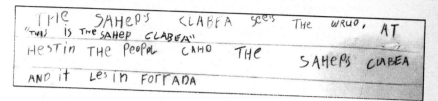

As an emergent reader, Joel can read books at the levels of "Step a Little Further" and "Step a Little Faster." Children like Joel require a shared reading experience in which you read those passages that are too difficult for them to manage alone. They are usually past the memorization stage, read pattern books easily, and are now ready to tackle, with some adult aid, books such as *The New Baby Calf*. Children's reading and writing develop in tandem, and our analysis of their written work helps us to coach their reading appropriately.

Chapter 5

Organizing the Classroom

How Do I Organize Space and Time in the Classroom?

Individualizing the reading and writing program often seems difficult to organize. What are all the other children doing while the teacher is holding personal reading and writing conferences? In this chapter we look at the physical organization of the room, the routines that the children follow, the storage and display of the books, and the way the teacher allocates time. These are all critical components of any successful program. The use of real books, literature, rather than prescribed reading schemes demands from teachers exactly these same considerations.

The first decision that must be made is how to organize your school day. The program that we are describing needs large blocks of time so that the children can pursue in depth a wide variety of activities related to literacy.

Picture the following Grade 1/2 classroom during the work period. Some children are independently illustrating a book they have just produced, others are involved with a challenge card in the sand, others are listening to a favorite tape, others are sharing a book with a friend, and still others are productively occupied with an open-ended mathematical challenge. Two girls have built a medieval castle using the large blocks and are writing invitations to knights to come to a tournament. At the art centre, four children are constructing a dragon from boxes and tissue paper that will hang from the ceiling. Two boys are sewing pillows in the shape of dragons. The teacher is sitting at a round table sharing a book with a child, while several other children are working at the table on their reading journals and their latest piece of writing. This is the classroom at work, not for half an hour during "centre" time but all day! This scene can be found in any classroom where there are four-, five-, six-, seven-, and eight-year-olds who are actively engaged in their learning. The only variation is, that as the age of the children increases, the complexity of their work will also increase.

The secret to the creation of such an idyllic scene is really quite simple. The stimulus comes from the books that we read and the topics we discuss. Then there must be large blocks of time for the children to become actively engaged in a wide variety of meaningful tasks, working in well-equipped and organized activity centres where materials can be found and used. Success depends upon our creating opportunities for the children to direct and select their own activities and learning objectives, establishing clear expectations for student behavior, and setting up simple, manageable routines.

Activity Centres

If our students are truly going to be given the opportunity to explore topics that interest them and to engage in tasks that will stimulate them to reflect, question, discuss, write, read, and seek new answers and understandings, the presence of permanent activity centres in our classrooms is vital. For any active learning program to run smoothly, the children must have easy, independent access not only to these permanent centres but also to any supplies that they might require to complete their projects. The teacher can't be sharing a book with a child and finding glue at the same time.

In our program we have established several such centres, complete with detailed but simple rules for use. Each centre has a labelled space for each article to make tidy-up easy. Monitors in the older grades can be responsible for checking that the supplies are replenished at the end of the day. The number of participants allowed at each centre is clearly noted by the number of chairs or by a sign.

The children well understand from frequent group discussions that before they start any new activity, they must first clean up their old work space and then discuss their new plans with us.

Permanent Centres That We Would Suggest

A Writing/Reading Table:

- complete with pencils, paper of various sizes and weights, erasers, staplers, tagboard or light cardboard for book covers, markers, colored pencils, rulers, and as many computers as you can find to use for composing.

A Dramatic Play Centre:

- which, depending on the teacher supplies, can change from a house, to a nursery, to a store, to a restaurant, to an office, to whatever the children decide. Remember to include paper and pencils for notes and books for interest, enjoyment, and information.

A Building Centre:

- complete with blocks of every size; a changing inventory of props – labelled buckets full of construction toys, small cars, people, animals, planes, and dinosaurs; and fabric, paper, pencils, and markers. This centre should be carpeted to help deaden some of the noise.

A Library Corner:

- cosy and inviting, filled with books of every kind, a record player/tape machine with earphones and tapes for quiet listening, pillows, a rug, and a rocking chair or two for easy reading, looking, and sharing.

A Craft Centre:

- that houses paper of every weight and color, glue that really sticks, scissors both left- and right-handed that really cut, material and found material such as small boxes, toilet-paper rolls, egg cartons, toothpicks, cotton balls, etc. To keep this centre tidy, try keeping the paper in a puzzle tray, the glue in plastic bottles stored in a work caddy with a handle for easy carrying, and all other materials in individually labelled buckets that stack.

A Paint Centre:

- that changes regularly to include new colors of paint or dye and different kinds of paint materials such as squirt paint, blow paint, finger paint, and soap paint for special projects. We like to keep our paints in special covered plastic jars that sit securely in a long tray. This unit is easily available from most school art-supply companies. The children paint either on an oilcloth on the floor or at an easel. Take your pick! Which method you use really depends on your physical space and equipment.

A Bin Toy Centre:

- that provides a wide variety of building toys such as Zaks, Lego, Tinkertoy, Small Blocks, and a train set – each in its own labelled bucket.

A Mathematics Centre:

- that provides a wide variety of manipulative materials for the children to use as they seek to make sense of the world of numbers, geometry, and measurement. Some suggested materials are measuring tapes, wheels, scales, pattern blocks, geoboards, counters of every size, color, and shape, chart paper, graph paper, and pencils. These materials will of course change according to the dictates of the unit of study at the time. Don't put out everything at once or chaos is sure to reign. Some of the equipment, such as blocks, counters, and measuring tools, should be easily available to the children at all times.

A Science Centre:

- complete with magnifying glasses, scales, books, and interesting collections to examine. We have found that collections of magnets, shells or batteries, and bulbs usually spark the interest of children of all ages. Be inventive about offering other collections for your students to explore.

A Sand and Water Centre:

- complete with two separate tables for the sand and water – recommended because they are such rich sources of language use and problem-solving activity. Include in this centre, as in all of the other centres, changing props to encourage the children to use new language, pose new questions, reflect on new learning, and offer new solutions. To make tidy-up easy, we always include a small hand-held whisk broom and dustpan for the sand and a bucket and several sponges for the water. Any additional props are stored on a table with each piece individually labelled. Small cars, people, dinosaurs, or animals are kept in individually labelled tubs.

These then are the permanent centres that we would suggest you establish in your room. Teachers have an enormous role to play in ensuring that these centres remain vital and exciting sources of learning. These centres, if they are to offer continual challenges to the children, must be constantly changed to reflect new class interests and to accommodate the children's developing skills.

The Theme Learning Centre

In addition to these permanent centres, we also provide a theme learning centre that acts as a resource for all the areas of study. Some popular themes that lend themselves to cross-disciplinary use are bears, dinosaurs, space, pets, me, etc. We change the themes as needed to meet the demands of the content curriculum prescribed by individual jurisdictions. Ideas for the theme can come from the teacher or the children.

The centre houses a collection of materials related to the theme, including fiction and nonfiction books, posters, interesting objects to examine and probe, puzzles, games, math challenges, and models. The permanent centres are used to extend this centre through art, writing, and building.

It is important to remember that reading and writing can occur at any of the centres in the room and should not be limited to designated areas. It is essential that the classroom offer a wide variety of changing tasks that provide opportunities to question, to discuss, to reflect, to write, and to read about subjects that interest each individual child.

Teachers often ask, But how do you find the *room* for all of these centres? Our solution, adopted by many of our colleagues, is simply to get rid of the individual desks that devour our classroom space. We find the children are quite content to live without a separate desk, if they have a chair at one of the many centres that they can call their own if they wish, and a personal bucket to hold their own special treasures. The centres, whether they are achieved by pushing the old desks together or scrounging low tables, become the focal point of the room; and because the sharing of resources is an intregal feature of these centres, the children have the opportunity to learn this important social skill through daily practice.

The Timetable

The other question we are frequently asked by our fellow teachers is, How do you organize the day so that these centres can be used productively and the curriculum covered? Our response is that there is no necessity to timetable centres. Most school days break down into four reasonably large blocks of time – two in the morning and two in the afternoon. Each block varies from 45 to 60 minutes, and although every situation and school is different, this is a basic schedule that gives children ample working time at any given centre. The centres provide an entirely suitable working environment for children to carry out independent study and co-operative, small-group projects.

Suggested Timetable for Half-day Morning Kindergarten Students

8:45 to 9:15	ENTRANCE/BOOK EXCHANGE
9:15 to 9:30	STORY/DISCUSSION
9:30 to 10:15	WORK PERIOD
10:15 to 10:30	TIDY-UP and SNACK TIME
10:30 to 10:45	PRIVATE BOOK TIME
10:45 to 11:00	STORY/MUSIC/BUDDY READING
11:00 to 11:30	OUTDOOR PLAY or WORK PERIOD
11:30 to 11:45	TIDY-UP
11:45	DISMISSAL

Suggested Timetable for Half-day Afternoon Kindergarten Students

1:00 to 1:15	ENTRANCE/BOOK EXCHANGE or PRIVATE READING TIME
1:15 to 1:30	STORY/DISCUSSION
1:30 to 2:30	WORK PERIOD

2:30 to 2:45	SNACK/MUSIC/STORY/BUDDY READING
2:45 to 3:00	BOOK EXCHANGE or PRIVATE READING TIME
3:00 to 3:30	OUTDOOR PLAY or WORK PERIOD
3:30	DISMISSAL

Suggested Timetable for Full-day Students

8:45 to 9:00	ENTRANCE/BOOK EXCHANGE
9:00 to 9:30	STORY/DISCUSSION
9:30 to 10:30	WORK PERIOD
10:30 to 10:45	RECESS
10:45 to 11:00	STORY/BUDDY READING
11:00 to 11:45	WORK PERIOD
11:45	DISMISSAL
1:00 to 1:20	ENTRANCE/PRIVATE READING TIME
1:20 to 1:30	STORY
1:30 to 2:30	WORK PERIOD
2:30 to 2:45	RECESS
2:45 to 3:15	WORK PERIOD
3:15 to 3:30	STORY/BUDDY READING

Chapter 6

Components of the Reading and Writing Program

How the Program Works on a Day-to-Day Basis

You've set up the activity centres, bought the books, and decided on the timetable. Now, what are the daily ingredients of a literature-based reading program? We have discussed how you share books with individual children, hold reading conferences, and make responses based on individual needs. What else is happening in the classroom?

The cornerstone is the daily sharing of books with the whole class.

1. Read Aloud

We read aloud two to four times daily, depending on whether the children attend school half-day or full-day. Reading first thing in the morning seems to set a positive tone for the day, and reading last thing in the afternoon helps end on an upbeat note. What do we read? EVERYTHING THAT WE FEEL CONSTITUTES GOOD LITERATURE. We share pattern books, big books, short novels, picture books, poetry, nonfiction material, favorite tales and, of course, the children's own writing. Why do we spend so much time reading? Well, some days it seems it's the only way to capture the attention of the group! There's nothing like the power of a story to calm an excited class. We also have critical objectives for this read-aloud time, however. We know that when we read aloud we have the opportunity to introduce children to wonderful stories and to hook them on the act of reading. By sharing our enthusiasm, we instill in them a love of books, model good reading behavior, and open up new and old areas for thought and reflection. In the read-aloud time we can introduce the children to more difficult text that is beyond their present reading ability. One of our favorites for Grade 1 and 2 students is Roald Dahl's *The Fantastic Mr. Fox*. Kindergarten children are held spellbound by Marianna Mayer's *The Black Horse*. We give them the opportunity to develop their skills in prediction and critical listening and thinking. We model for the children how we want them to listen to others' opinions and how to question. We encourage them to defend their responses.

This read-aloud time often precedes the children's work period, and therefore we can take the opportunity to suggest activities that will link the story with their play, their writing, and their art. Janet and Allan Ahlberg's story *The Jolly Postman* inspired Eric, Karl, and Dinesh, a group of five-year-olds, to make a series of postcards to send when they took a voyage in their submarine, made the previous day in the block centre. Robert Munsch's *The Paper Bag Princess* sparked Dino, George, Emma, and Sofia, a group of five- and six-year-olds, to make paper-bag princesses, princes who were "stuck up," and fierce dragons. This group of children eventually used their puppets to make a play for their classmates. The reading of Carol and Donald Carrick's story *Patrick's Dinosaurs* inspired Amy, Daphne, Alexander, and Josh to begin simple research projects on what actually happened to the dinosaurs. This topic eventually expanded to include endangered animals and environments.

It is also a time to suggest other titles that the children might like to read on their own or with one of their reading buddies. This is a very precious part of the day, and we *never* let it be squeezed out of the timetable.

2. Individual Reading Time

Once the children have heard a story read aloud they often want to read it by themselves. Of course they find it easier to read when they have heard it before. This individual reading practice is a very important component of our language program.

We schedule time each day for the children to spend privately with a book. This time can be first thing in the morning, after recess, or first thing in the afternoon. The length of time varies with the age of the children. For a class of four- and five-year-olds this might be no more than 5 to 10 minutes, while children in Grade 3 might read for 20 minutes. The whole class sits in a large circle. Each child chooses a book from a collection brought to the middle of the circle. As teachers we change this selection to reflect the changing needs of the class. We make a conscious effort to include books that address the interests or theme of the moment. We also make available new materials and old favorites borrowed from the school library. Reading at this time for the youngest children may simply mean looking at the pictures. We do not require these children to record their selections. Children from the beginner reading stage onward are requested to write at least one or two words from the title of the book in their reading log.

This whole-class reading time gives us the opportunity to observe, to chat with one or two children about what they are reading, and to read ourselves. In addition to this whole-class reading time, the book corner is available during the work period for further private reading for all the children to enjoy.

3. Buddy Reading

As well as hearing stories read aloud by the teacher and reading by themselves, children in the kindergarten and primary grades need to share books with other people as often as possible. One of the ways of providing more of this critical listening time is to start a Buddy Reading program. This is an interclass program that teams up more fluent and usually older readers with beginning readers. We find this program works most successfully when a number of conditions are in place.

- Limit this sharing to three times a week. If you do it too often it loses its impact and disrupts other programs.
- Timetable this program immediately before or after recess.
- Confine the reading locations to the library, either of the two classrooms, and the halls.

- Set a time limit of 15 minutes. Many of the children enjoy this time so much that they will spend hours, if they are allowed, actively engaged in this shared reading.
- Monitor the selection of books carefully so that the young children select books that they can read with little difficulty. Do not put the older children in the position of "teacher." Their role is to be an interested listener.
- Hold miniworkshops with the listeners to help them be effective. Stress that when their buddy stumbles on a word, they should *tell them the word.* Caution them against overcorrecting the child and suggest that if their buddy makes many errors, they simply *take over the reading* and tell us later what happened.
- Insist that both partners record their choice of material in their joint reading log.

TITLE	READER	COMMENT
The boy in the drawer	Pashalia	we like the part when she turned on the cold water
A hippopopotamos ate the teacher	Pashalia	we liked the part when it ate the teacher.
Jimmy's boa bounces back	Pashalia	we both like the note book we also thought that was funny.
Angry Arthur	Pashalia	when he made the earth like a giant cracking egg.
The Story of Ferdinand	Pashalia	When Ferdinand sat in the middle of the stadium and smelt the flowers
Coco can't wait	Pashalia	when they past each other and didn't meet.
The tiny tiny woman	Pashalia	we like the part when she said take it.
busy nights	Katie	we liked the part when they had a party
I know an old lady	Katie	we liked the part when she swallowed the horse
The bath	Katie	we liked when she was playing in the mud.
new blue shoes	Katie	we liked when she asked if she could trade feet.
The patch work cat	Katie	we liked when the milk man found her.

The success of Buddy Reading programs depends upon the collaboration of the two teachers involved and the school librarian. We must talk to each other regularly, modify the program to suit the needs of both groups of children, and constantly encourage the children to share their responses and experiences as buddy readers.

4. Borrow-a-Book

Another way to immerse the children in stories is to start a Borrow-a-Book program.[10] This is an out-of-school reading program in which the children share books with their families. Books are borrowed on a daily basis and the parents and children read together. To begin:

- Make a special bag for each child. Bags can be constructed out of waterproof oilcloth with a shoulder strap and a Velcro fastener at the top to keep out the rain and the snow. The results are worth the trouble; these special bags not only give this program status but also make it easy to identify the children's book bag. This can really help a busy family in the morning!

- Include a ***comment booklet*** that has space to record the title of the book to be shared, the name of the reader, and comments from both the reader and the listener. Comments might include how the sharing went, whether they enjoyed the reading, and what other books they might like.

But may be I didn't give it my full concentration. The story is sterile, flat: it has no soul." Jane

"Right on!"

Title	Reader	Comment
The Lady and the Unicorn		I haven't read this. The illustrations are quite rich. The story is quite simple, but it's a nice enough fairy tale. The illustrations really are beautiful.

[10] Linda Hart-Hewins and Jan Wells, *Borrow-a-Book: Your Classroom Library Goes Home* (Richmond Hill, Ontario: Scholastic-TAB Publications, 1988).

Title	Reader	Comment
Feeding Babies		I haven't read either of these books. How are they? Emma liked the elephants best. I liked the hippos. It's a sweet book.
Little Witch's Big Night		E. loves stories about witches. In this book, a few kids get to have a ride on a broomstick. Loads of fun!
Buggy Riddles		Do you like silly riddles?: I know Emma does. She enjoyed this book even tho she didn't get many of the jokes - I like silly riddles too, even Emma's.
Carousel		Wildsmith is an amazing artist! We all loved this book.

- Try to respond to these comments so that a channel of communication between home and school can be opened.
- Do regular in-service sessions with parents to ensure that they understand the purposes of the program. They are to listen to the child's reading in a positive manner, not overcorrecting and not afraid to take up the reading if the book is too difficult for the child.
- Monitor the books to be shared. As with the senior buddy readers, we do not want these listeners put in the position of being the teacher.

Borrow-a-Book has many unexpected bonuses. Children see their parents and their teacher working together on something that both feel is important. Reading is seen to be valued both at home and at school.

The Buddy Reading and Borrow-a-Book programs help us provide time for our students to read individually to an interested, more fluent reader. These programs also have another important use. They offer a ready-made opportunity for children to *listen* to stories on an individual basis. We use these programs to provide the time that all children require if they are to develop a love of stories. Thus we encourage our school and home buddies to alternate this sharing time so that our students take on the roles both of listener and reader. In those homes where English is not read, we encourage the children to tell their parents the story, talk about the pictures, and read very simple, familiar pattern books.

We also provide some mother-tongue books because we want

our students to hear stories in a language with which the reader feels at ease. We want this to be an enjoyable time, not a test of endurance.

We hold miniworkshops both for the parents and for the older students about how to read effectively, how to question, and how to select the books to be shared. These two programs are very successful and have helped turn our classrooms into an environment where books literally take over. The children cannot get enough of their stories. They become very knowledgeable about their preferred authors and the kind of stories they like. They have taken to hiding their favorite books, putting them on reserve, as it were, to share with their home and school reading buddies. Favorite books are shared many, many times. There is always a stack of books that have been recommended by the children, waiting to be read.

5. Daily Writing Opportunities

Daily opportunities to write are also a crucial part of the language program. As they encode their own words in print, the children learn about the shapes and sounds of letters and words. They turn to the books they have read to find out how to spell words they need. Books are the source of much of their knowledge about print.

Yet a literature-rich classroom offers the child more than just concepts about print. Literature provides the stepping stone for their progress as writers. There are writerly ways of telling stories that differ from everyday oral language, and it is the children's experience of literature that introduces them to this more formal language. As Margaret Meek says, it is the texts that teach.[11]

Books offer children ideas for their own personal writing, models to copy as they seek to put their ideas down on paper, and answers to the many questions they need to address as they write on nonfiction topics. We feel it is critical that children be given abundant opportunities to write in some fashion every day. For children as for adults, writing is a process through which they attempt to produce a document that reflects their thinking,

---

[11]Margaret Meek, *How Texts Teach What Readers Learn* (Stroud, Gloucester: The Thimble Press, 1988).

their beliefs, and their knowledge. The children's knowledge of books and their various styles help these budding authors find a voice that suits the ideas they wish to convey to an audience.

Creating pattern books is favored by young children. Initially we read a number of pattern books to the group and/or listen to an individual child share such a book with us. We examine with the children the characteristics of the pattern, such as its repeating or rhyming elements. At this point we might suggest that the children make their own pattern books, using this form but selecting a topic that is of interest to them. Thus George at Halloween wrote "Ghost, ghost, what do you see? I see a monster looking at me... Monster, monster what do you see? I see a vampire looking at me..."

After hearing a series of fairy tales read to the class, a group of five girls decided to retell their favorite of the lot. *Hansel and Gretel* was their choice. Considerable time was spent by this group deciding the order of the retelling and who would produce which picture and accompanying text. The children took special care to vary their illustrative style to suit the text of each part of the story. So the happy parts were done in bright bold colors, and the sad parts were done in dark scratchy colors.

What to Do With Reluctant Writers?

Our response to such a query is to counter with a question of our own: Why does the child not want to write? Is it because the child has difficulty forming the letters? If this is the case, we would suggest the use of a computer. If this is not possible, consider sharing the task of writing with the child. Have the child begin the composition, and when you see he or she is tiring take over the task yourself. Continue on in this manner until the story is completed.

Another technique that we have used very successfully with these children is to pair them with children who have no problem putting pen to paper. The composition is a shared endeavor. A buddy writing system, whereby an older child scribes for the younger writer, is also an effective strategy to use with children whose fine motor skills are slow to develop.

For the child who says, "I don't know what to write about!" there are many strategies that can be employed. A technique that has worked very well for us is to have the children make a list of all the areas in which they think they are an expert. Everyone thinks they are an expert at something! From this list the children are able to select a topic that they can begin to research.

Teaming the children with a writing partner is another strategy that we have used to full advantage. Writing partners listen to initial ideas, offer practical and sensitive suggestions, act as a critical but supportive audience for first drafts, and help edit final drafts for publishing.

To keep track of the children's progress in writing we use writing folders, two for each child. One is for current work and is kept in a hanging file folder near the writing table. Each piece of work is dated, and any conference notes or changes in the children's print literacy that we have observed are noted on the back of the work. When the children are finished a piece of writing, we store it in another file folder that is kept in a filing cabinet. These finished pieces of work form the basis for our reporting to parents and the program evaluations that we regularly make for each child. A TIP – BUY A DATE STAMP AND KEEP THE WORK IN DATED SEQUENTIAL ORDER SO THAT IT IS EASIER TO SEE ANY PATTERN THAT MIGHT BE DEVELOPING !

Any writing that goes home does so in the form of a book, properly edited and published. This alleviates the problem of parents seeing unedited work and inappropriately compelling the children to correct it.

Chapter 7

A Portrait of a Primary Classroom in Action

How Literature Becomes the Spark for Learning

The story that follows is an account of how one theme developed in the classroom program. Language activities were fully integrated with many of the other curriculum areas. Furthermore, many activities took place simultaneously with children working individually or in small groups. The activities that the children engaged in involved listening, speaking, reading, writing, art, drama, building, and problem solving.

A theme might be inspired by a story shared as a group, a trip planned by the teacher, a special celebration, an important event in the news or in a child's life, or a school initiative. Children and teacher regularly plan together what is to be learned, when this learning will take place, and how the activities will be carried out. It is our opinion that this is the basis for true interactive and child-centred education. The children are key voices in the discussion about the specific activities, projects, writing, and reading that are to be undertaken in the upcoming weeks.

The following theme began one bright clear sunny morning in February when the teacher read the thought-provoking new picture book by Celia Godkin, *Wolf Island,* to her class of five-, six-, and seven-year-olds.

This beautiful true story sparked a lively discussion that led to many different activities, stories, thoughts, and play. The children were fascinated by the realization that if one element of the environment is removed (the wolves), the rest of the environment (plants, animals, and people) suffers.

The children were keen to find out more about what causes animals to die.

The classroom theme centre provided a starting point for their research; their intense curiosity soon had them looking further afield. At work time a group of children scurried off to the school library where, assisted by the teacher-librarian, they developed an expanded list of books on animals and the environment. They returned to the classroom with their arms full.[12]

Over the next few weeks the class shared these books during the regular read-aloud times. They included *Rain Forest* by Helen Cowcher, *Antarctica* by the same writer, Jeannie Baker's *Where the Forest Meets the Sea,* Bill Peet's *Farewell to Shady Glade*, and *The Accident* by Carol Carrick.

Other children on that first day took on the responsibility of searching their own library corner for other stories and books that could be examined in more depth. Over the next weeks they spent many enjoyable and informative hours poring over books such as Betty Waterton's *A Salmon for Simon, Frogs* by John Williams, *Our World Is in Danger* by Gillian Dorfman, and *Endangered Animals* by Lynne Stone. After reading *Patrick's Dinosaurs* and *What Happened to Patrick's Dinosaurs?* by Carol and Donald Carrick, one boy made the connection between the plight of the dinosaurs and the current state of endangered species. Barbara Smucker's *Jacob's Little Giant* and Roald Dahl's *The Fantastic Mr. Fox* held the class spellbound for many days as they waited to hear who would triumph – man or animal.

The sand centre became the site of Wolf Island for three five-year-olds. After much discussion and sand pushing, they designed an island in the middle of the table. This was surrounded by blue tissue paper to signify the water. They raided the Plasticine supplies and spent many days poring over books

---

[12] Most of the books cited in this chapter were collected by the children from the school library to develop their theme. They are not part of our classroom theme unit library and so do not appear in our *Real Books for Reading* bibliography. Publishing information for these titles appears at the end of this chapter.

so that all the animals would "look right." The wolves were shown on a raft floating away from the island. The raft was constructed from parts of the connect building set. To ensure that this centre remained untouched past the work session, a sign was devised asking that other students DNT TAJ. At the end of this very involved project, the children agreed that labels were required for all the animals. They said, "We need signs so when people come when we're not here they'll know what the animals are. We also better put our names on this so they know we did it." Another group of children made a poster to hang over this project, warning people of the dangers of tampering with the environment. They also insisted on signing their names.

The play with the building materials also began to reflect the growing interest in the theme. After hearing the story *Antarctica,* one group of six- and seven-year-olds decided to build Antarctica complete with mountains, the sea, animal life, and oil rigs. This project took several days and involved trips to the library to search out books that clearly showed not only what Antarctica looks like but also what animals and sea creatures live there. The animals were made from Plasticine, felt, fur, and found materials. The land and sea were made by covering a round table with papier-mâché. Mountains and valleys were formed by using boxes and mounds of newspaper under the mâché. One boy took it upon himself to make several oil rigs from Lego. Again, these children labelled all their work because this was important if they were to share their knowledge with another class.

Several children drew and painted pictures about animals in their natural habitats. They were encouraged to write three facts they knew about the animal they had chosen. Then their task was to visit the library and find out if their animal was in any way threatened by extinction. This became a mini-research project. The individual reading conference time with the teacher was spent finding the relevant information and unlocking its meaning. The teacher found that because much of the nonfiction material was at a higher reading level than the children could easily manage by themselves, she had to share the reading task. At one point the demand for help with reading became so great that she introduced these books both into the Borrow-a-Book and the Buddy Reading programs. The parents were asked to help the children find the answers to their specific questions. The buddy readers also read books about animals and shared their knowledge of endangered species. The quest for information led the children to tackle books normally considered too difficult for them. With their strong sense of purpose and the support of teachers, parents, and friends, these children extended their reading skills. They learned new words by sight, used letter clues to sound out new words, and looked at pictures to aid their reading. The process of learning to read was deeply embedded in the research project.

The big blocks became the site of many different kinds of "endangerment" play. On one occasion two children were on a whaling ship. Their mission was "to get whales." Two other children were in a much smaller Greenpeace ship; their job was "to stop the bad guys." The teacher suggested that the children make some props to assist their play. These props were quite clever and time-consuming to create. Over the course of several days the children made harpoons out of long tubes, a packed lunch from the plastic food in the house, rain jackets from the dress-up centre, and walkie-talkies out of two boxes and string. In between times the whaling ships became safari jeeps in Africa. Their occupants were out looking for elephant poachers. Other days the block play had nothing to do with the theme, but in every instance the teacher encouraged the children to extend their play, to add props, to make signs, and to share their work with their classmates.

The story **Rain Forest** by Helen Cowcher inspired a gorgeous mural of the rain forest itself. Most of the children contributed to this activity. The background was created by using sponges and a wide array of paint colors. Once the background effect was achieved, other children made the trees, vines, and animals. To give the mural texture and depth, the children used several different techniques to make the animals and foliage. Some made their animals by sewing or gluing fabric into appropriate shapes and then stuffing them. Other children made two-dimensional animals from papier-mâché and tissue paper. Still others used a crushed tissue-paper technique. The foliage and trailing vines were crafted from crushed paper. Once the mural was finished, the children made a sign that said SV THE RAN FREST.... PLES....

The class brainstormed to come up with suggestions for saving the environment. A group of the older children put these ideas on a poster for the whole school to share. They also brainstormed for insights into the factors that cause the environment and animals to be threatened. These ideas were put into a book with assistance from the reading buddies; it became an interclassroom project. These books were housed in the school library for all the children in the school to share.

The group became so enthused about saving the animals that they held a bake sale to raise money to help adopt an animal at the Metropolitan Toronto Zoo. The children wrote a letter to their parents explaining the reason for the bake sale and asking for their help. It was strongly suggested that the parents only assist with or supervise the baking and *not* do it for the child. Posters were made to advertise the sale and invitations were sent to all the classes in the school. At every turn the children explained why they were having a sale.

The theme of animals, their habitats, and their state of endangerment took over the talk, the reading, the writing, the artwork, and the play for several weeks. Not all the children worked on every task, but each child did contribute to one of the many projects. As this theme was unfolding in the room, there were of course many other individual themes developing. Not all of the children were interested in this one topic all of the time. They had their own interests, their own questions, and their own projects to pursue. The teacher respected this need and only asked that over the course of the week all children read with an adult, share their writing with an adult, discuss their projects with an adult, and share the finished product with their peers.

This theme was so successful that the class decided to invite their parents and friends to applaud their work. They held an open house during the day that stretched on into the early evening. Each child stood with his or her own work to answer any questions that the viewers might have. Tao proudly showed the filmstrip that he had made depicting the animals of the Arctic and their state of endangerment. Sarah shared her research book on the rain forest and expertly answered questions about how to buy an acre of it. Evan and Nick worked the tape-recorder and showed slides of pictures that they had made. They told about all the different kinds of endangerment there are in the world today.

They even offered their own solutions to these problems. Families, school personnel, and the children all enjoyed this sharing of knowledge and the celebration of a job well done.

During the course of this theme the children had the opportunity to contribute their own ideas for art projects, play activities, reading research, and writing. Looking back, it is possible to see how the theme had evolved – not because the teacher had decided in advance what was to be done, but because she had a clear view of the learning objectives, had provided the resources, and had made the classroom a place in which children could experiment and work. Literature had been the spark and was used at all stages of the learning. The writing that went on during these weeks was motivated by genuine interest in the topic. The personal reading that took place was also motivated by the children's intense desire to learn more. They represented their learning in many ways and as they used language to learn, so they learned more about how to use language. Themes such as this one allowed the children, their teacher, and their families to learn together about a topic of common interest and relevancy.

There are, however, some practical issues to be addressed if this form of thematic learning is to be successful. How the children and teacher decide what work is to be accomplished on any given day is critical.

To ensure that everyone works productively, the teacher uses a one-to-one approach. All the children are asked in turn what work they have to finish or what task they wish to begin that day. A negotiation process follows, in which both the teacher and the student agree what work is to be accomplished. It is our opinion that children must have some say in how they spend their day if they are to be truly engaged in the act of learning. The ability to select an area of interest for study, to accept the responsibility for that learning, and to get on with the task at hand are life skills that children must be given abundant opportunities to practise and master. We do our children no good if we make all their decisions for them.

It is also during this individual negotiation process that the teacher takes the opportunity to set up times to share a book with the child, to discuss the latest writing or reading project, or to assign a specific task to be accomplished at the building centre, the sand and water centre, the craft table, or in the dramatic play centre. This time provides the teacher with an overview of the status of the class. A simple *tracking sheet* can be checked each day to provide a record of which children are going to which centres. These sheets allow the teacher to see patterns emerging and report more accurately to parents about their children's choices.

Activities. (first choice) a.m. Sk's.	Writing/Drawing	Crafts	Paints	Blocks/Building	Sand/Water	Library	Dramatic Play	Math	Science	Reading with Me	Big Toys/Puzzles	Interest Centre – Celebrations
Week of Dec 4 → 8												
Aileen	X		X				X X	.		:		X directed
Susan		XX				X				directed X	X	
Nicole	(project) XXX					X				X		
Denise		XX	X	X	X						X	
Amy	XX	X		XX			X					
Sofia					X	XX		X				X
Nick			X	X		X					X	X
Tomas	X			XX						X		XX
John								X	X	X		

The way that the teacher spends his or her time in such a classroom is also critical. The majority of my time is spent either circulating about the room offering assistance where needed, or at the writing/reading table as the beginning readers and writers share stories and compose their own writing. The writing centre is an excellent position from which to survey the room, to spot frustrations as they occur, to encourage children to stay on task, and to hold those innumerable miniconferences that are so necessary in an active learning environment. A TIP – SIT WITH YOUR BACK TO THE WALL SO YOU CAN EASILY SEE THE WHOLE ROOM AT A GLANCE.

If teachers are to be involved in and informed about the individual children's progress, it is necessary that they hold a miniconference with each student as each task is completed. This is an opportunity to congratulate them on their work, seek clarification about their plans, offer new challenges, record their activities, and arrange for them to share their work with their peers if they wish to do so.

The teacher also spends time talking with a number of children on a more in-depth level. Realistically, it is only possible to hold a conference with six to eight children a day. This is the context in which we assist the reading and writing development of these children – coaching, mediating, encouraging, and keeping track of their individual progress.

Conclusions

Does this approach to the teaching and learning of reading and writing really work? Our reply to this question is an emphatic *yes*. Our experience in our classrooms convinces us that if we make reading a meaningful, enjoyable, and frequent experience for children, they will read not because they have to, but because they want to. They will then be well on their way to becoming literate in the full sense of the word. We cannot make reading meaningful or enjoyable without real books. Real books for reading are essential for success.

Footnotes for Chapter 7

Theme-development books cited in this chapter are:

Celia Godkin, *Wolf Island* (Fitzhenry & Whiteside, 1989).
Helen Cowcher, *Rain Forest* (A. Deutsch, 1988) and *Antarctica* (A. Deutsch, 1990).
Jeannie Baker, *Where the Forest Meets the Sea* (Greenwillow Books, 1987).
Bill Peet, *Farewell to Shady Glade* (Houghton Mifflin, 1966).
Carol Carrick, *The Accident* (Seabury Press, 1976).
John Williams, *Frogs* (Puffin, 1989).
Gillian Dorfman, *Our World Is in Danger* (World Wildlife Fund, Ladybird Ltd., 1989).
Lynn M. Stone, *Endangered Animals* (Chicago Childrens Press, 1984).
Barbara Smucker, *Jacob's Little Giant* (Kestrel, 1987).

Real Books for Reading
Bibliography

This book list is a selection of children's literature that has been used and approved by children. It is intended to support teachers who wish to use real books in their early-reading programs.

It is by no means intended to be prescriptive. We offer it as a guide for those teachers who may want to buy more literature for their classrooms or add books to their school library which will be available for reading programs. Clearly, it represents a personal selection; we hope that teachers will find it a useful starting point, and that to every category they will add their own titles.

We have listed books which are currently in print and available in North America. For books that are available through additional or different publishers in the United States, we have noted the relevant publishing information in brackets.

Please note that we have supplied publishing information for the *paperback* editions wherever possible. The reason for this is simple—paperbacks are cheaper than hardcover books, so we can buy more of them. A literature-rich classroom can *never* have too many books!

Wordless Picture Books

Aruego, José. *Look What I Can Do*. Scribner, 1971.
(Macmillan, 1988.)

Briggs, Raymond. *The Snowman*. Hamilton, 1978.
(Faber & Faber, 1987. Random, 1988.)

Goodall, John S. *Adventures of Paddy Pork*.
Harcourt Brace Jovanovich, 1968.

—*The Story of a Castle*. André Deutsch, 1987.
(Macmillan, 1986.)

Hughes, Shirley. *Up and Up*. Penguin, 1981. (Lothrop, 1986.)

Mayer, Mercer. *A Boy, a Dog, and a Frog*. Dial Books for
Young Readers, 1979.

Mayer, Mercer and Mayer, Marianna. *A Boy, a Dog, a Frog,
and a Friend*. Doubleday, 1978.

McCully, Emily Arnold. *School*. Harper & Row, 1987.

—*Picnic*. Harper & Row, 1989.

Ormerod, Jan. *Sunshine*. Kestrel Books, 1981.
(Penguin, 1984.)

—*Moonlight*. Kestrel Books, 1982. (Penguin, 1984.)

Prater, John. *The Gift*. Viking Kestrel, 1986. (Penguin, 1987.)

Sasaki, Isao. *Snow*. Viking, 1982.

Spier, Peter. *Peter Spier's Rain*. Doubleday, 1987.

Turkle, Brinton. *Deep in the Forest*. Dutton, 1976.

Poetry and Nursery Rhymes

Agard, John. *I Din Do Nuttin and Other Poems*. Magnet, 1984.

Bennett, Jill and Oxenbury, Helen. *Teeny Tiny*. Putnam, 1986.

Briggs, Raymond. *Fee Fi Fo Fum*. Penguin, 1969.

—*The Mother Goose Treasury*. Penguin, 1973. (Dell, 1986.)

Degen, Bruce. *Jamberry*. Harper & Row, 1985.

Downie, Mary Alice and Robertson, Barbara (eds.) Illus. by
Elizabeth Cleaver. *The New Wind Has Wings*.
Oxford University Press, 1987.

Greenfield, Eloise. *Honey, I Love and Other Love Poems*.
Harper & Row, 1986.

Heidbreder, Robert. Illus. by Karen Patkau.
Don't Eat Spiders. Oxford University Press, 1987.

King, Karen. Oranges and Lemons.
Oxford University Press, 1987.

Kovalski, Maryann. *The Wheels on the Bus*.
Kids Can Press, 1988.

Lee, Dennis. *Garbage Delight*. Macmillan, 1977.

—*Alligator Pie*. Macmillan, 1981.

—*Jelly Belly*. Macmillan, 1983. (Bedrick Books, 1985.)

Lobel, Arnold. *The Random House Book of Mother Goose*.
Random House, 1986.

Lobel, Arnold and Prelutsky, Jack. *The Random House Book of Poetry for Children*. Random House, 1983.

Prelutsky, Jack. *The New Kid on the Block*. Greenwillow, 1984.

—*Read Aloud Rhymes for the Very Young*. Knopf, 1986.

—*Ride a Purple Pelican*. Greenwillow, 1986.

Raffi. *One Light One Sun*. Crown, 1987.

Reid, Barbara. *Sing a Song of Mother Goose*.
Scholastic Inc., 1989.

Rosen, Michael. *You Can't Catch Me*. Penguin, 1983.

—*Don't Put Mustard in the Custard*.

—*When Did You Last Wash Your Feet?* André Deutsch, 1986.

Silverstein, Shel. *Where the Sidewalk Ends*.
Harper & Row, 1974.

—*A Light in the Attic*. Harper & Row, 1981.

Stones, Rosemary and Mann, Andrew. *Mother Goose Comes to Cable Street*. Penguin, 1980.

Watson, Clyde. *Catch Me and Kiss Me and Say It Again*.
Collins, 1978. (Putnam, 1983.)

—*Father Fox's Pennyrhymes*. Harper & Row, 1987.
(Scholastic Inc., 1975.)

Williams, Sarah. *Round and Round the Garden: Fingerplay Rhymes for the Very Young*. Oxford University Press, 1983.

Concept Books

Ahlberg, Janet and Allan. *The Baby's Catalogue*. Penguin,
1984. (Little, Brown, 1986.)

—*Yum Yum*. Viking Kestrel, 1984.

Barton, Byron. *Where's Al?* Clarion Books, 1972.
(Houghton Mifflin, 1989.)
Boyle, Alison. *Counting Surprises. – Alphabet Surprises*.
MacDonald, 1987.
Burningham, John. *First Words*. Walker Books, 1984.
—*Wobble Pop. – Cluck Baa. – Sniff Shout. –Slam Bang. –
Jangle Twang*. Walker Books, 1984. (Penguin, 1985.)
—*Numbers Book*. Walker Books, 1988.
Crews, Donald. *Truck*. Penguin, 1985.
—*Harbor*. Morrow, 1987.
—*Flying*. Greenwillow, 1989.
—Other titles available.
Ehlert, Lois. *Color Zoo*. Lippincott, 1989.
(Harper & Row, 1989.)
Emberley, Rebecca. *Jungle Sounds. – City Sounds*.
Little, Brown, 1989.
Gretz, Susanna. *Teddybears 1-10*. Collins Picture Lions, 1973.
(Macmillan, 1986.)
—*Teddybears ABC*. Collins Picture Lions, 1980.
(Macmillan, 1986.)
Hoban, Tana. *I Read Signs*. Mulberry, 1983. (Morrow, 1987.)
—*What Is It? – One, Two, Three*. Greenwillow, 1985.
—*Panda Panda*. Greenwillow, 1986.
—*Over, Under and Through*. Macmillan, 1986.
Hughes, Shirley. *Lucy and Tom's A.B.C.* Gollancz, 1984.
(Penguin, 1987.)
Hutchins, Pat. *One Hunter*. Penguin, 1980. (Greenwillow,
1982.)
Maris, Ron. *My Book*. Penguin, 1986.
Ormerod, Jan. *Reading. – Sleeping*. Walker Books, 1985.
(Lothrop, 1985.)
Oxenbury, Helen. *I Touch – I Hear. – I See. – I Can*.
Walker Books, 1985. (Random, 1985.)
Numbers of Things. –ABC of Things. Collins Picture
Lions, 1987. (Delacorte, 1983.)
Pienkowski, Jan. *Colors. – Shapes. – ABC*. Penguin, 1983.
(Simon and Schuster, 1989.)
—*Homes. – Weather. – Sizes. – Time*. Penguin, 1983.
(Messner, 1983.)
—*Numbers. – Faces*. Penguin, 1983.
—*Zoo. – Farm*. Penguin, 1983. (David & Charles, 1985.)

Wood, A. J. *Animal Opposites*. Templar, 1987.
Ziefert, Harriet. *Cock-a-Doodle-Doo! – All Clean! – All Gone! – Run! Run!* Harper & Row, 1986.

Pattern Books

Asch, Frank. *I Can Blink. – I Can Roar*. Kids Can Press, 1985. (Crown, 1986.)
Barton, Byron. *Where's the Bear?* Penguin, 1984.
Campbell, Rod. *Dear Zoo*. Penguin, 1987. (Macmillan, 1988.)
—*Oh Dear!* Piper Books, 1989. (Macmillan, 1986.)
Gomi, Taro. *Shadows*. Heian International, 1981.
Hawkins, Colin. *What's the Time, Mr. Wolf?* Collins Picture Lions, 1985.
Hawkins, Colin and Jacqui. *I Know an Old Lady Who Swallowed a Fly*. Little Mammoth, 1989.
Hill, Eric. *Where's Spot?* (and other titles). Putnam, 1980. (Interlink, 1988.)
Maris, Ron. *Better Move On, Frog*. Collins, 1984.
Martin, Bill Jr. and Carle, Eric. *Brown Bear, Brown Bear, What Do You See?* Holt Rinehart, 1983. (Henry Holt, 1983.)
Nichol, b.p. *Once: A Lullaby*. Black Moss Press, 1983. (Greenwillow, 1986.)
Rees, Mary. *Ten in a Bed*. Little Mammoth, 1989. (Little, Brown, 1988.)
Roffey, Maureen. *Home Sweet Home*. Pan, 1985. (Putnam, 1983.)
Stobbs, William. *Gregory's Dog*. Oxford University Press, 1987.
Tafuri, Nancy. *Have You Seen My Duckling?* Penguin, 1986. (Greenwillow, 1984.)
Wildsmith, Brian. *Cat on the Mat. – All Fall Down.– Toot Toot. – What a Tale*. Oxford University Press, 1987.
Wood, Leslie. *A Dog Called Mischief. – Bump, Bump, Bump*. Oxford University Press, 1987.
Ziefert, Harriet and Smith, Mavis. *Going on a Lion Hunt*. Penguin, 1989.

First Steps

Ahlberg, Allan and McNaughton, Colin. Rednose Readers (Red Series): *Help! – Jumping. – Make a Face. – Big Bad Pig. –Fee Fi Fo Fum. – Bear's Birthday. – So Can I*. Random House, 1985.

Barton, Byron. *Building a House*. Penguin, 1984. (Greenwillow, 1981.)

—*Airport*. Penguin, 1986. (Harper & Row, 1987.)

—*Trucks*. Penguin, 1986. (Harper & Row, 1986.)

—*I Want to Be an Astronaut*. Scholastic Inc., 1989. (Harper & Row, 1988.)

Bayley, Nicola. *Polar Bear Cat. – Parrot Cat. – Elephant Cat.– Crab Cat. – Spider Cat*. Walker Books, 1988. (Knopf, 1984.)

Browne, Anthony. *I Like Books*. Walker Books, 1988. (Knopf, 1989.)

—*Things I Like*. Walker Books, 1989. (Knopf, 1988.)

Bruna, Dick. *I Can Read*. Methuen, 1969.

Burningham, John. *The Snow. – The School.– The Rabbit. –The Baby. – The Friend. – The Blanket. – The Cupboard. –The Dog*. Jonathan Cape, 1983. (Harper & Row, 1976.)

Dodds, Siobhan. *Elizabeth Hen. – Charles Tiger*. Collins Picture Lions, 1989. (Little, Brown, 1988.)

Drawson, Blair. *I Like Hats*. Scholastic Inc., 1980.

Galdone, Paul. *Three Little Kittens*. Clarion Books, 1986.

Garland, Sarah. *Doing the Washing*. Penguin, 1984.

—*Going Shopping. – Having a Picnic*. Penguin, 1986.

—*Coming to Tea*. Penguin, 1987.

Gomi, Taro. *Spring Is Here*. Fitzhenry & Whiteside, 1989. (Chronicle Books, 1989.)

Grindley, Sally. *Four Black Puppies*. Walker Books, 1987. (Lothrop, 1987.)

Hunia, Fran. *Oops*. Ashton Scholastic, 1984.

Inkpen, Mick. *If I Had a Pig*. Macmillan, 1988. (Little, Brown, 1988.)

Isadora, Rachel. *I Touch*. Collins Picture Lions, 1987. (Greenwillow, 1985.)

Lingren, Barbro and Erikssen, Eva. *Sam's Car. – Sam's Biscuit.– Sam's Teddy*. Methuen, 1984.

Maris, Ron. *Are You There, Bear?* Penguin, 1986.
(Greenwillow, 1985.)

McKee, David. *Not Now, Bernard*. Beaver Books, 1987.
(Penguin, 1986.)

Ormerod, Jan. *Dad's Back. – Messy Baby*. Walker Books,
1985. (Lothrop, 1985.)

Riddell, Chris. *Ben and the Bear*. Walker Books, 1986.
(Harper & Row, 1986.)

Roffey, Maureen. *Look, There's My Hat!* Pan, 1986.
(Putnam, 1985.).

Taylor, Judy and Cartwright, Reg. *My Dog. – My Cat*.
Walker Books, 1987. (Macmillan, 1989).

Titherington, Jeanne. *Pumpkin, Pumpkin*. Greenwillow, 1986.

Ward, Leila. *I Am Eyes Ni Macho*. Scholastic Inc., 1987.

Watanabe, Shigeo. *How Do I Eat It?* Penguin, 1982.
—*Hello, How Are You?* Penguin, 1984.
—*I'm Going for a Walk*. Penguin, 1986.

Wildsmith, Brian. *The Island. – If I Were You*.
Oxford University Press, 1987.

Wolff, Ashley. *Only the Cat Saw*. Penguin, 1988.
(Putnam, 1985.)

Wood, Leslie. *The Frog and the Fly. – Tom and His Tractor*.
Oxford University Press, 1987.

Step a Little Further

Ahlberg, Allan and McNaughton, Colin. Rednose Readers
(Yellow Series): *Crash Bang Wallop! – Me and My Friends.
– Push the Dog. – Shirley's Shops*. Random House, 1985.

Asch, Frank. *Just Like Daddy*. Prentice-Hall, 1981.

Breinburg, Petronella. *My Brother Shawn*. Penguin, 1986.

Brown, Ruth. *A Dark Dark Tale*. Hippo Books/Scholastic,
1985. (Dial Books for Young Readers, 1984.)

Bruna, Dick. *I Can Read More*. Methuen, 1969.
(Price Stern, 1984.)

Carle, Eric. *The Very Hungry Caterpillar*. Penguin, 1974.
(Putnam, 1986.)

Donnelly, Liza. *Dinosaur Day*. Scholastic Inc., 1987.

Ginsburg, Mirra. *Three Kittens*. Crown, 1973.
—*Where Does the Sun Go at Night?* Mulberry, 1981.
(Greenwillow, 1980.)
—*The Chick and the Duckling*. Macmillan, 1988.
Ginsburg, Mirra and Tafuri, Nancy. *Across the Stream*.
Penguin, 1985. (Greenwillow, 1982.)
Gomi, Taro. *Coco Can't Wait*. Penguin, 1985.
Harper, Anita and Hellard, Susan. *It's Not Fair*. Penguin,
1986. (Putnam, 1986.)
—*Just a Minute!* Penguin, 1987. (Putnam, 1987.)
Hayes, Sarah. *This Is the Bear*. Walker Books, 1986.
(Harper & Row, 1986.)
Hutchins, Pat. *Rosie's Walk*. Collins, 1968. (Macmillan, 1971.)
—*Good-Night Owl*. Penguin, 1975. (Macmillan, 1972.)
—*Happy Birthday, Sam*. Penguin, 1981. (Greenwillow, 1978.)
—*You'll Soon Grow Into Them, Titch*. Penguin, 1985.
(Greenwillow, 1983.)
Jones, Maurice. *I'm Going on a Dragon Hunt*. Penguin, 1988.
(Macmillan, 1987.)
Kraus, Robert and Aruego, José. *Whose Mouse Are You?*
Collins, 1970. (Macmillan, 1972.)
—*Where Are You Going, Little Mouse?* Mulberry, 1986.
(Morrow, 1989.)
Levinson, Riki and Goode, Diane. *I Go With My Family to
Grandma's*. Dutton, 1986.
Lewis, Tracey. *Where Do All the Birds Go?* Dutton, 1988.
Lung, Earlene. *Gone Fishing*. Houghton Mifflin, 1984.
Maris, Ron. *I Wish I Could Fly*. Penguin, 1988.
(Greenwillow, 1987.)
Piers, Helen. *Hamster Is Hiding. – Kittens in the Kitchen.
–Puppy in the Park. – Goat in the Garden* (and other titles).
Methuen, 1984.
Rockwell, Anne. *Boats*. Dutton, 1985.
—*Toolbox*. Penguin, 1982. (Macmillan, 1971.)
Rockwell, Harlow. *My Nursery School*. Penguin, 1974.
Rose, Gerald. *Ahh! Said Stork*. Picturemac, 1986.
Watanabe, Shigeo. *How Do I Put It On?* Penguin, 1981.
(Putnam, 1984.)
—*I'm the King of the Castle!* Penguin, 1984. (Putnam, 1982.)
—*I Can Build a House!* Penguin, 1985. (Putnam, 1985.)
—*I'm Playing With Papa!* Penguin, 1986.

Wildsmith, Brian. *Giddy Up*. Oxford University Press, 1987.

Ziefert, Harriet. Hello Reading! Series: *Nicky Upstairs and Down. – Harry Takes a Bath. – Mike and Tony: Best Friends*. Penguin, 1987.

Step a Little Faster

Ahlberg, Janet and Allan. *Each Peach Pear Plum*. Collins, 1980. (Penguin, 1986.)

Allen, Pamela. *Who Sank the Boat?* Hamish Hamilton, 1982. (Putnam, 1985.)

Asch, Frank. *The Last Puppy*. Prentice-Hall, 1983.

Bang, Molly. *Ten, Nine, Eight*. Penguin, 1985. (Greenwillow, 1983.)

Bonsall, Crosby. *Mine's the Best*. Harper & Row, 1984.

Brown, Margaret Wise and Hurd, Clement. *Goodnight Moon*. Harper & Row, 1977.

Brown, Ruth. *The Big Sneeze*. Collins, Beaver Books, 1986. (Lothrop, 1985.)

Burningham, John. *Mr. Gumpy's Motor Car*. Penguin, 1983. (Harper & Row, 1976.)

—*Come Away From the Water, Shirley*. Collins, 1983. (Harper & Row, 1983.)

—*Mr. Gumpy's Outing*. Penguin, 1984. (Henry Holt, 1971.)

—*Would You Rather...* Collins, 1984. (Harper & Row, 1978.)

Chase, Edith Newlin and Reid, Barbara. *The New Baby Calf*. Scholastic Inc., 1986.

Chorao, K. *Kate's Car. – Kate's Box. – Kate's Snowman. – Kate's Quilt*. Dutton, 1982.

Eastman, P. D. *Are You My Mother?* Collins, 1962. (Random, 1967.)

Ginsburg, Mirra and Barton, Byron. *Good Morning, Chick*. Scholastic Inc., 1980. (Greenwillow, 1980.)

Goodspeed, Peter. *A Rhinoceros Wakes Me Up in the Morning*. Penguin, 1984.

Gray, Nigel and Craig, Helen. *The One and Only Robin Hood*. Walker Books, 1987. (Little, Brown, 1987.)

Joyce, William. *George Shrinks*. Harper & Row, 1987.

Kraus, Robert. *Herman the Helper.* Windmill Books, 1974. (Simon and Schuster, 1987. Prentice-Hall, 1987.)

Kraus, Robert and Aruego, José. *Leo the Late Bloomer.* Windmill Books, 1971. (Harper & Row, 1987.)

Krauss, Ruth. *The Carrot Seed.* Harper & Row, 1945.

Lottridge, Celia Barker. *One Watermelon Seed.* Oxford University Press, 1987.

Mayer, Mercer. *There's a Nightmare in My Closet.* Dial Books for Young Readers, 1976.

McPhail, David. *Fix-It.* Unicorn, 1987. (Dutton, 1984.)

Natanani, Chiyoko. *Feeding Babies.* Penguin, 1983.

Nicoll, Helen and Pienkowski, Jan. *Meg and Mog.* Penguin, 1976.

—*Meg's Eggs. – Meg's Castle.* Penguin, 1975.

—*Mog's Mumps.* Penguin, 1979. (David & Charles, 1983.)

—*Mog at the Zoo.* Penguin, 1985.

—*Owl at School.* Penguin, 1986. (David & Charles, 1984.)

—Other titles available.

O'Connor, Jane. *The Teeny Tiny Woman.* Step-Into-Reading: Random House, 1986.

Polushkin, Maria. *Mother, Mother, I Want Another.* Crown, 1986.

Pomerantz, Charlotte; Aruego, José; and Dewey, Ariane. *One Duck, Another Duck.* Penguin, 1984. (Greenwillow, 1984.)

Rice, Eve. *Sam Who Never Forgets.* Penguin, 1980. (Greenwillow, 1977. Morrow, 1987.)

Shaw, Nancy. *Sheep in a Jeep.* Houghton Mifflin, 1988.

Stadler, John. *Hooray for Snail!* Harper & Row, 1985.

Stinson, Kathy. *Red Is Best.* Annick Press, 1982. (Firefly Books, 1982.)

—*Big or Little.* Annick Press, 1983. (Firefly Books, 1983.)

Sutton, Eve. *My Cat Likes to Hide in Boxes.* Penguin, 1978.

Wells, Rosemary. *Noisy Nora.* Dial Books for Young Readers, 1980.

Wildsmith, Brian. *What the Moon Saw.* Oxford University Press, 1978.

Taking Off

Ahlberg, Janet and Allan. *Peepo!* Penguin, 1983.

Asch, Frank. *Sand Cake*. Parents Magazine, 1987. (Crown, 1987.)

Blake, Quentin. *Mister Magnolia*. Collins, 1987.

Bonsall, Crosby. *Who's Afraid of the Dark?* Harper & Row, 1985.

Brandenberg, Franz. *I Don't Feel Well*. Penguin, 1982.

Browne, Anthony. *Through the Magic Mirror*. Picturemac, 1987.

Carle, Eric. *The Secret Birthday Message*. Harper & Row, 1986.

DeMorest, Chris L. *Benedict Finds a Home*. Methuen, Pocket Bears, 1984.

de Paola, Tomie. *The Knight and the Dragon*. Putnam, 1980.

Falconer, Elizabeth. *Three Little Witches*. Collins Picture Lions, 1989.

Hearn, Emily and Collins, Heather. *Whoosh! I Heard a Sound*. Annick Press, 1983.

Hoff, Syd. *Danny and the Dinosaur*. Harper & Row, 1978.

—*The Horse in Harry's Room*. Harper & Row, 1985.

Hurd, Edith Thacher. *Johnny Lion's Book*. Harper & Row, 1985.

Hutchins, Pat. *Tom and Sam*. Penguin, 1972.

—*Don't Forget the Bacon!* Penguin, 1982. (Greenwillow, 1976. Morrow, 1989.)

Keats, Ezra Jack. *Over in the Meadow*. Scholastic Inc., 1971.

Lobel, Arnold. *Mouse Tales*. Harper & Row, 1978.

—*Frog and Toad Are Friends*. Harper & Row, 1979.

—*Owl at Home*. Harper & Row, 1982.

—*Days With Frog and Toad*. Harper & Row, 1984.

Mahy, Margaret. *Seventeen Kings and Forty-Two Elephants*. Collins Picture Lions, 1979. (Dial Books for Young Readers,1987.)

Minarik, Else. *A Kiss for Little Bear* (and other titles). Harper & Row, 1968.

Murray, Jill. *Peace at Last*. Dial Books for Young Readers, 1980.

Oram, Hiawyn and Kitamura, Satoshi. *Angry Arthur*. Penguin,1984. (Dutton, 1989.)

Pinkwater, Daniel. *I Was a Second Grade Werewolf*. Dutton, 1985.

Ross, Tony. *I'm Coming to Get You!* Dial Books for Young Readers, 1987.

Thaler, Mike. *There's a Hippopotamus Under My Bed*. Avon Books, 1978.

—*A Hippopotamus Ate the Teacher*. Avon Books, 1981.

—*Upside Down*. Avon Books, 1986.

You're Away

Ahlberg, Allan. *Happy Families* (series, 12 titles). Penguin/ Kestrel Books, 1981.

—*Funnybones*. Collins, 1982. (Greenwillow, 1981.)

Bonsall, Crosby. *The Case of the Cat's Meow*. Harper & Row, 1978.

Browne, Anthony. *Gorilla. – A Walk in the Park*. Methuen, 1985. (Knopf, 1985.)

—*Willy the Wimp*. Methuen, 1986. (Knopf, 1985.)

Carlson, Nancy. *Harriet and the Garden* (and other titles). Penguin, 1985.

Cohen, Miriam and Hoban, Lillian. *When Will I Read?* (and other titles). Dell, 1987.

Freeman, Don. *Corduroy*. Penguin, 1976.

—*A Pocket for Corduroy*. Penguin, 1978.

Giff, Patricia Reilly and Natti, Susanna. *Today Was a Terrible Day*. Penguin, 1980.

Gilman, Phoebe. *Jillian Jiggs*. Scholastic Inc., 1988.

Hautzig, Deborah. *Little Witch's Big Night*. Step-Into-Reading: Random House, 1987.

Hurd, Thacher. *Mama Don't Allow*. Harper & Row, 1985.

Keats, Ezra Jack. *The Snowy Day*. Penguin, 1976.

—*Whistle for Willie*. Penguin, 1977.

—*Peter's Chair*. Harper & Row, 1983.

Mahy, Margaret. *The Boy Who Was Followed Home*. Dial Books for Young Readers, 1983.

McNulty, Faith. *The Elephant Who Couldn't Forget*. Harper & Row, 1989.

McPhail, David. *Snow Lion*. Parents Magazine, 1987.
(Crown, 1987.)

Munsch, Robert. *The Dark*. Annick Press, 1979. Firefly Books
(Canada and the U.S.), 1984.

Nicklaus, Carol. *That's Not Chester*. Avon Books, 1975.

—*Harry the Hider*. Avon Books, 1979.

Rice, Eve. *New Blue Shoes*. Penguin, 1979.

Sendak, Maurice. *Where the Wild Things Are*. Harper & Row,
1988.

Stinson, Kathy and McLoughlin, Mary. *Those Green Things*.
Annick Press, 1985. (Firefly Books, 1985.)

On Your Own at Last

Brandenberg, Franz. *Nice New Neighbors*. Scholastic Inc.,
1980. (Greenwillow, 1977.)

Briggs, Raymond. *Jim and the Beanstalk*. Penguin, 1973.
(Putnam, 1989.)

Briggs, Raymond and Vipont, Elfrida. *The Elephant and the
Bad Baby*. Penguin, 1971.

Carle, Eric. *The Grouchy Ladybug*. Harper & Row, 1986.

Carrick, Carol and Donald. *Patrick's Dinosaurs*.
Clarion Books, 1982. (Houghton Mifflin, 1983.)

—*What Happened to Patrick's Dinosaurs?* Clarion Books,
1984. (Ticknor & Fields, 1986.)

Emberley, Barbara. *Drummer Hoff*. Prentice-Hall, 1967.

Fox, Mem. *Wilfrid Gordon McDonald Partridge*. Penguin,
1987. (Kane-Miller Books, 1989.)

Gerstein, Mordicai. *Arnold of the Ducks*. Harper & Row, 1985.

Hayes, Sarah and Ormerod, Jan. *Eat Up, Gemma*.
Walker Books, 1988. (Lothrop, 1988.)

Hoberman, Mary Ann and Fraser, Betty. *A House Is a House
for Me*. Penguin, 1982.

Marshall, Edward. *Fox and His Friends*. Dial Books for
Young Readers, 1982.

—*Fox All Week*. Dial Books for Young Readers, 1987.

Mayer, Mercer. *What Do You Do With a Kangaroo?*
Scholastic Inc., 1975.

Munsch, Robert. *The Paper Bag Princess*. Annick Press, 1980. Firefly Books (Canada and the U.S.), 1980.
—*Love You Forever*. Firefly Books (Canada and the U.S.), 1982.
—*Millicent and the Wind*. Annick Press, 1984. Firefly Books (Canada and the U.S.), 1984.
—*Thomas' Snowsuit*. Annick Press, 1985. Firefly Books (Canada and the U.S.), 1985.
Peppé, Rodney. *The Mice Who Lived in a Shoe*. Penguin, 1984. (Lothrop, 1982.)
—*The Kettleship Pirates*. Penguin, 1985.
Rylant, Cynthia. *When I Was Young in the Mountains*. Dutton, 1985.
Staunton, Ted and Kovalski, Maryann. *Puddleman*. Kids Can Press, 1983.
Stren, Patti. *Hug Me*. Fitzhenry & Whiteside, 1977. (Harper & Row, 1984.)
Thurman, Mark. *Two Pals on an Adventure* (series).
—*Douglas the Elephant* (series). NC Press, 1985.
Ungerer, Tomi. *The Three Robbers*. Atheneum Children's Books, 1962. (Macmillan, 1975.)
Wagner, Jenny. *John Brown, Rose and the Midnight Cat*. Penguin, 1980.
Wayne von Konigslow, Andrea. *That's My Baby*. Annick Press, 1986.
Yolen, Jane. *Commander Toad in Space* (and other titles). Coward McCann, 1984. (Putnam, 1980.)
Zion, Gene. *Harry the Dirty Dog*. Harper & Row, 1976.

Getting Longer

Ahlberg, Janet and Allan. *Burglar Bill*. Collins, 1979.
—*The Jolly Postman*. Heinemann, 1986. (Little, Brown, 1986.)
Alexander, Sue. *World Famous Muriel. – World Famous Muriel and the Scary Dragon*. Dell, 1988.
Aliki. *We Are Best Friends*. Mulberry, 1982. (Greenwillow, 1982.)
Allard, Harry. *Miss Nelson Is Missing*. Houghton Mifflin, 1985.
Aubin, Michel and Desputeaux, Hélène. *The Secret Code*. James Lorimer & Co., 1987.

Blades, Ann. *Mary of Mile 18*. Tundra Books, 1971.

Blake, Quentin. *Patrick*. Penguin, 1970.

Blume, Judy. *The One in the Middle Is the Green Kangaroo*. Dell, 1982. (Bradbury, 1981.)

—*The Pain and the Great One*. Dell, 1985. (Bradbury, 1984.)

Burningham, John. *Where's Julius?* Collins, 1988. (Crown, 1987.)

Carrier, Roch. *The Hockey Sweater*. Tundra Books, 1984.

Castor, Harriet. *Fat Puss and Friends*. Penguin, 1985.

Christian, Mary Blount. *Swamp Monsters*. Dial Books for Young Readers, 1983.

Cohen, Barbara. *The Carp in the Bathtub*. Kar-Ben Copies Inc., 1987.

Cohen, Miriam and Hoban, Lillian. *Liar, Liar, Pants on Fire!* Dell, 1987. (Greenwillow, 1985.)

—*See You Tomorrow, Charles*. Dell, 1989. (Greenwillow, 1983.)

Cooney, Barbara. *Miss Rumphius*. Penguin, 1985.

Doppert, Kursa and Monika. Trans. by Karen Englander. *The Streets Are Free*. Annick Press, 1985.

Edwards, Dorothy. *My Naughty Little Sister Goes Fishing*. Penguin, 1985.

Foreman, Michael. *Dinosaurs and All That Rubbish*. Penguin, 1974.

—*Long Neck and Thunderfoot*. Penguin, 1984.

—*War and Peas*. Penguin, 1987. (Harper & Row, 1974.)

Havill, Juanita. *Jamaica's Find*. Houghton Mifflin, 1986.

Hughes, Shirley. *Dogger*. Collins Picture Lions, 1979. (Lothrop, 1988.)

—*Moving Molly*. Collins Picture Lions, 1981. (Prentice-Hall, 1982. Lothrop, 1988.)

—*Alfie Gets in First*. Collins Picture Lions, 1982. (Lothrop, 1982.)

—*Alfie's Feet*. Collins Picture Lions, 1984. (Morrow, 1988.)

—*Alfie Gives a Hand*. Collins Picture Lions, 1985. (Morrow, 1986.)

Kellog, Steven. *The Island of the Skog*. Dial Books for Young Readers, 1976.

Kovalski, Maryann. *Brenda and Edward*. Kids Can Press, 1984.

Leaf, Munro. *The Story of Ferdinand*. Penguin, 1988.

Lewis, Thomas P. *Hill of Fire*. Harper & Row, 1983.

Monjo, F. N. *Drinking Gourd*. Harper & Row, 1983.

Munsch, Robert. *Mud Puddle*. Annick Press, 1982. Firefly Books (Canada and the U.S.), 1982.

—*David's Father*. Annick Press, 1983. Firefly Books (Canada and the U.S.), 1983.

Munsch, Robert and Kusugak, Michael. *A Promise Is a Promise*. Annick Press, 1987. Firefly Books (Canada and the U.S.), 1988.

Peet, Bill. *The Ant and the Elephant*. Houghton Mifflin, 1980.

Potter, Beatrix. *The Tale of Peter Rabbit*. Frederick Warne, 1902.

Rockwell, Anne and Harlow. *The Night We Slept Outside*. Macmillan, 1986.

Rey, H. A. *Curious George*. Houghton Mifflin, 1973.

Rose, Gerald. *The Tiger Skin Rug*. Penguin, 1981.

Ryan, John. *Pugwash and the Midnight Feast. – Pugwash and the Wreckers*. Penguin, 1986.

Sharmat, Marjorie Wienman. *Nate the Great* (and other titles). Dell, 1977. (Putnam, 1972.)

Steig, William. *Sylvester and the Magic Pebble*. Windmill Books, 1969. (Simon and Schuster, 1988.)

—*Amos and Boris. – The Amazing Bone*. Penguin, 1977. (Farrar, Straus & Giroux, 1971, 1976.)

—*Dr. de Soto*. Scholastic Inc., 1982. (A Sunburst Book, Farrar, Straus & Giroux, 1982.)

—*Gorky Rises*. A Sunburst Book, Farrar, Straus & Giroux, 1986.

Turkle, Brinton. *Do Not Open*. Dutton, 1985.

Van Allsburg, Chris. *The Wreck of the Zephyr*. Houghton Mifflin, 1983.

Varley, Susan. *Badger's Parting Gifts*. Collins Picture Lions, 1985. (Lothrop, 1984.)

Waterton, Betty. *A Salmon for Simon*. Douglas & McIntyre, 1987.

Wells, Rosemary. *Timothy Goes to School*. Dial Books for Young Readers, 1983.

Wildsmith, Brian. *The Little Wood Duck*. Oxford University Press, 1987.

Yeoman, John and Blake, Quentin. *Mouse Trouble*. Penguin, 1976.

Zolotow, Charlotte. *William's Doll. – My Grandson Lew*. Harper & Row, 1985.

First Novels

Adler, David A. *The Fourth Floor Twins and the Skyscraper Parade*. Penguin, 1988.

—*Cam Jensen and the Mystery of the U.F.O.* (and other titles). Dell, 1982. (Penguin, 1980.)

Aiken, Joan. *Fog Hounds, Wind Cat, Sea Mice*. Piccolo, 1987.

Ardizzone, Edward and Aingelda. *The Little Girl and the Tiny Doll*. Young Puffin, 1979.

Berends, Polly. *The Case of the Elevator Duck*. Random House, A Stepping Stone Book, 1989.

Blume, Judy. *Freckle Juice*. Dell, 1978.

—*Superfudge*. Dell, 1981.

Brown, Jeff. *Flat Stanley*. Methuen, 1980. (Harper & Row, 1964.)

Buck, Pearl S. *The Big Wave*. Harper & Row, 1986.

Bulla, Clyde Robert. *A Lion to Guard Us*. Scholastic Inc., 1983. (Harper & Row, 1989.)

Cameron, Ann. *Julian's Glorious Summer*. Random House, A Stepping Stone Book, 1987.

—*The Most Beautiful Place in the World*. Knopf, 1988.

—*Julian, Secret Agent*. Random House, A Stepping Stone Book, 1988.

—*The Stories Julian Tells*. Knopf, 1989.

Coerr, Eleanor. *The Josefina Story Quilt*. Harper & Row, 1986.

Coombs, Patricia. *Dorrie and the Haunted House* (and other titles). Dell, 1980.

Coville, Bruce and Katherine. *Sarah's Unicorn*. Harper & Row, 1985.

Cresswell, Helen. *Dragon Ride*. Penguin, 1987.

Dahl, Roald. *The Magic Finger*. Penguin, 1974. (Harper & Row, 1966.)

—*Roald Dahl's Revolting Rhymes*. Penguin, 1984. (Bantam, 1986.)

—*The Fantastic Mr. Fox*. Penguin, 1988. (Bantam, 1978.)

Erickson, Russell. *Warton and Morton*. Dell, 1977.

Fox, Paula. *Maurice's Room*. Macmillan, 1988.

Gannett, Ruth Stiles. *The Dragons of Blueland*. Knopf, 1963.

—*My Father's Dragon. – Elmer and the Dragon*. Knopf, 1987.

Heide, Florence Parry. *The Shrinking of Treehorn*. Penguin, 1971. (Holiday, 1971. Dell, 1979.)

Hughes, Shirley. *It's Too Frightening for Me*. Penguin, 1986.

—*Chips and Jessie*. Fontana Young Lions, 1985. (Lothrop, 1986.)

Hutchins, Pat. *The House That Sailed Away*. Fontana, 1975. (Greenwillow, 1975.)

Laurin, Anne. *Perfect Crane*. Harper & Row, 1987.

MacLachlan, Patricia. *Sarah Plain and Tall*. Harper & Row, 1985.

—*Seven Kisses in a Row*. Harper & Row, 1988.

Moore, Lilian and Adelson, Leone. *The Terrible Mr. Twitmeyer*. Scholastic Inc., 1988.

Parish, Peggy. *Amelia Bedelia* (and other titles). Scholastic Inc., 1970. (Harper & Row, 1983.)

Proysen, Alf. *Little Old Mrs. Pepperpot*. Beaver Books, 1984. (ABC-Clio, 1989.)

Rayner, Mary. *Mrs. Pig Gets Cross and Other Stories*. Collins, 1986.

Rosen, Michael. *Hairy Tales and Nursery Crimes*. Fontana Young Lions, 1987.

Shrub, Elizabeth. *The White Stallion*. Bantam, 1984.

Smucker, Barbara. *Jacob's Little Giant*. Penguin, 1987.

Wallace, Ian. *The Sandwich*. Kids Can Press, 1975.

Whelan, Gloria. *Next Spring an Oriole*. Random House, 1987.

White, E. B. *Stuart Little*. Harper & Row, 1945.

Williams, Margery. *The Velveteen Rabbit*. Avon Books, 1982.

Yeoman, John. *The Boy Who Sprouted Antlers*. Fontana Young Lions, 1987.

Traditional Tales

Aardema, Verna. *Why Mosquitoes Buzz in People's Ears*. Atheneum Children's Books, 1980. (Dial Books for Young Readers, 1978.)

—*Bringing the Rain to Kapiti Plain*. Picturemac, 1983. (Dial Books for Young Readers, 1983.)

Bang, Molly. *Dawn*. Morrow, 1983.

—*The Paper Crane*. Mulberry, 1987. (Morrow, 1987.)

Blegvad, Erik. *The Three Little Pigs*. Prentice-Hall, 1980. (Macmillan, 1980.)

de Paola, Tomie. *Strega Nona's Magic Lessons*. Prentice-Hall, 1975. (Harcourt Brace Jovanovich, 1984.)

—*The Legend of the Bluebonnet: An Old Tale of Texas*. Putnam, 1983.

Ehrlich, Amy and Jeffers, Susan. *Thumbelina*. Dial Books for Young Readers, 1985.

Galdone, Paul. *The Gingerbread Boy*. Houghton Mifflin, 1983.

Haley, Gail. *A Story, a Story*. McClelland & Stewart, 1970.

Hastings, Selina. *Sir Gawain and the Loathly Lady. – Peter and the Wolf*. Walker Books, 1987. (Lothrop, 1985.)

Kipling, Rudyard. *The Elephant's Child*. Harcourt Brace Jovanovich, 1988.

Le Cain, Errol. *Thorn Rose*. Penguin, 1978.

Mayer, Marianna. *The Black Horse*. Dial Books for Young Readers, 1987.

Mayer, Mercer. *East of the Sun and West of the Moon*. Four Winds Press, 1980. (Macmillan, 1986.)

Mosel, Arlene. *Tikki Tikki Tembo*. Scholastic Inc., 1968. (Henry Holt, 1989.)

—*The Funny Little Woman*. Dutton, 1972.

Muller, Robin. *Tatterhood*. Scholastic-TAB, 1984. North Winds Press, 1984.

Rockwell, Anne. *The Three Bears and Fifteen Other Stories*. Harper & Row, 1984.

Seuling, Barbara. *The Teeny Tiny Woman*. Penguin, 1978.

Stern, Simon. *The Hobyahs*. Methuen, 1983.

Tolstoy, Alexei and Oxenbury, Helen. *The Great Big Enormous Turnip*. Pan, 1982.

Wildsmith, Brian. *The Hare and the Tortoise*. Oxford University Press, 1982.

Williams, Jay and Mayer, Mercer. *Everyone Knows What a Dragon Looks Like*. Four Winds Press, 1976. (Macmillan, 1976.)

Wolkstein, Diane. *The Banza*. Dial Books for Young Readers, 1984.

Zernach, Margot. *The Little Red Hen*. Penguin, 1986.

Further Professional Reading

Atwell, Nancie. *In the Middle: Writing, Reading and Learning With Adolescents*. Portsmouth, New Hampshire: Boynton/Cook, 1987.

Barton, Bob and Booth, David. *Stories in the Classroom*. Toronto: Pembroke Publishers, 1989. Portsmouth, New Hampshire: Heinemann (U.S.), 1989.

Bennett, Jill. *Learning to Read With Picture Books*. 3rd ed. Stroud, Gloucester: The Thimble Press, 1988.

Booth, David; Swartz, Larry; and Zola, Meguido. *Choosing Children's Books*. Toronto: Pembroke Publishers, 1987.

Butler, Dorothy. *Babies Need Books*. London: Pelican Press, 1984.

—*Five to Eight*. London: The Bodley Head, 1986.

Chambers, Aidan. *Introducing Books to Children*. 2nd ed. London: Heinemann, 1983. Boston: Horn Book (U.S.), 1983.

—*Booktalk: Occasional Writing on Literature for Children*. London: The Bodley Head, 1985.

Clay, Marie. *Reading: The Patterning of Complex Behaviour*. 2nd ed. Portsmouth, New Hampshire: Heinemann, 1980.

Cullinan, Bernice E., ed. *Children's Literature in the Reading Program*. Newark, Delaware: International Reading Association, 1987.

Goodman, Kenneth. *What's Whole in Whole Language?* Richmond Hill, Ontario: Scholastic, 1986. Portsmouth, New Hampshire: Heinemann (U.S.), 1986.

Graves, Donald H. *Writing: Teachers and Children at Work*. Portsmouth, New Hampshire: Heinemann, 1983.

Hart-Hewins, Linda, and Wells, Jan. *Borrow-a-Book: Your Classroom Library Goes Home*. Richmond Hill, Ontario: Scholastic-TAB Publications, 1988.

Hazard, Paul. *Books, Children and Men*. Boston: The Horn Book, 1944. 5th ed. (U.S.), 1983.

Landsberg, Michele. *Michele Landsberg's Guide to Children's Books*. Markham, Ontario: Penguin Books Canada, 1985.

Meek, Margaret. *Learning to Read*. London: The Bodley Head, 1982. Portsmouth, New Hampshire: Heinemann (U.S.), 1986.

—*How Texts Teach What Readers Learn*. Stroud, Gloucester: The Thimble Press, 1988.

Meek, Margaret et al. *The Cool Web: The Pattern of Children's Reading*. London: The Bodley Head, 1977.

Smith, Frank. *Reading Without Nonsense*. New York: Teachers College Press, 1985.

Taylor, Denny and Strickland, Dorothy. *Family Storybook Reading*. Portsmouth, New Hampshire: Heinemann, 1986.

Trelease, Jim. *The Read-Aloud Handbook*. Harmondsworth, Middlesex: Penguin, 1985. Peter Smith (U.S.), 1984. Penguin (U.S.), 1984.

Tucker, Nicholas. *The Child and the Book*. Cambridge: Cambridge University Press, 1981.

Villiers, Una. *Luk Mume Luk Dade I Kan Rit*. Richmond Hill, Ontario: Scholastic, 1989.

Waterland, Liz. *Read With Me: An Apprenticeship Approach to Reading*. Stroud, Gloucester: The Thimble Press, 1985.

Weaver, Constance. *Reading Process and Practice: From Socio-Psycholinguistics to Whole Language*. Portsmouth, New Hampshire: Heinemann, 1988.

Wells, Gordon. *The Meaning Makers*. Portsmouth, New Hampshire: Heinemann, 1986.

Woodward, Virginia; Harste, Jerome; and Burke, Carolyn. *Language Stories and Literacy Lessons*. Portsmouth, New Hampshire: Heinemann, 1984.